# QUESTIONS FOR GOD

LeRoy Lawson

COLLEGE PRESS PUBLISHING CO., Joplin, Missouri

Second Printing, 1992

Printed and Bound in the
United States of America


International Standard Book Number: 0-89900-414-8

# TABLE OF CONTENTS

*INTRODUCTION* .......................................... 7

*1. WHY IS THERE SUFFERING IN THE WORLD?* .... 11

*2. WILL THERE EVER BE A CURE FOR ALL DISEASES?* .................................. 25

*3. WHY IS THERE EVIL IN THE WORLD?* ........... 39

*4. WILL THERE EVER BE LASTING WORLD PEACE?* ................................ 51

*5. WILL MAN EVER LOVE HIS FELLOW MAN?* ...... 65

*6. WHEN WILL THE WORLD END?* .................. 79

*7. WHAT DOES THE FUTURE HOLD?* ............... 91

*8. IS THERE LIFE AFTER DEATH?* ..................105

*9. WHAT IS HEAVEN LIKE?* ..........................119

*10. HOW CAN I BE A BETTER PERSON?* .............131

# INTRODUCTION:
## Of The Asking Of Questions There Is No End

If you could ask God any question you want, what would it be? I formulated my request many years ago, after attempting for some time to accomplish this nearly impossible thing called marital adjustment. "When I die and go to heaven," I have told any audience that would listen, "I'm going to ask God, 'Why, when You made us male and female, did You put in different thermostat settings?' " Having thought on the subject more deeply with the passing years, I'd now have to add a second: "Why, as we grow older, do the settings keep moving farther and farther apart?"

Your question would investigate the mysteries of the universe much more seriously than mine, I'm certain. So would mine, actually. In fact, you and I would probably seek solutions to some of the puzzlers posed in this book. They are universal.

The ten questions raised here came from the published results of a Christian Broadcasting Network survey several years ago. I didn't learn of it firsthand; a friend told me that CBN had asked a representative sampling of non-Christian Americans what question they would ask God if they could. The ten most frequently raised were then published. Having once read the list my friend sent me, I couldn't stop thinking about the survey. Eventually I raised the questions with my congregation in a ten-week sermon series, and again in our home Bible study groups.

I wish I could tell you that now, at long last, after the world's greatest minds have failed to provide satisfactory answers, my congregation and I have produced a book that will put your mind at ease once and for all.

We haven't and it won't. The quest will continue. We have uncovered little you haven't already found out for yourself.

You may wonder why I've bothered writing, then, if I have so little new to contribute. It's a fair question.

Let me defend myself. This book is designed for group study, like the home Bible studies in our church. You'll find questions at the end of each chapter, and some scriptures for further thought. My hope is that what I've written will stimulate good discussion, acting as a catalyst to trigger deeper personal meditation and the exchange of thoughtful insights into the purposes of God.

While I haven't solved the riddles, I have tried to direct our attention to some of their implications. These questions arise out of our humanness; Christians and non-Christians wonder about the same things. Their answers are often different, but perhaps not as different as is often supposed. To be humanly alive is to wonder, to question, to doubt, to probe, to overcome, and finally to assert.

Sometimes Christians succumb to the temptation to jump too quickly to the final step. They assert before they question; they claim victory before they fairly hear all sides. They seize a few scriptural truths without dealing with opposing scriptural truths. Shouting "Christ is the Answer," they betray an ignorance of the real question. As a result, they are often written off as bigoted, fearful, unthinking religionists who claim to know the truth when in fact they've really never pursued it. And, even worse, because of prominence of some of these shouters, Christianity in general is sometimes dismissed as a body of anti-intellectuals who can't cope in the real world of ideas.[1]

As I hope I will make clear, the Christian can honestly answer the questions raised here, although not always with a simple yes or no. He will sometimes fail to persuade to his position either the rigid fundamentalist on the one hand or the secular humanist on the other. He seeks the firm middle ground, believing the sovereign God is still in charge of the universe and human beings are neither gods nor kings of all they survey. They live in a less than predictable world; they can know some things but not everything. They still must walk by faith.

My approach in these chapters is meditative, suggestive, and non-authoritative. You won't find definitive answers here, and you'll quickly sense that, unlike Christ, I do not speak as one having authority. I am in effect doing with you what I hope you will do with others in group discussion. I'm making my contribution to the debate, offering some opinions (they may sound like prejudices), inviting your rebuttal, and trusting that when we have finished listening to one another we'll all be wiser.

You must not think that I confuse my ruminations with the inspired writings. I don't. They are tentative thoughts offered by a Christian pilgrim in mid-journey. I reserve the right to have my mind changed, to be taught the way of the Lord more perfectly, perhaps by you. What I offer here does not define orthodoxy; it doesn't even define me. On some of the issues, I may change my mind tomorrow, with new evidence.

My favorite question is the last one. The essential glory of the Christian faith is not to be found in its institutions, its heritage or traditions, its promises of an afterlife, but in a person, Jesus Christ, and the magnificent promises it offers, that a person like me might, through His power at work within me, become like Him.

Many people want to become better.

Christians have been given the way to do it.

### Endnotes

**1.** The scriptures, on the other hand, urge us to careful study of both God's world and God's word. See Psalm 119; Matthew 22:29; Acts 17:11; 18:24-26; Romans 1, I Timothy 4:11-13; II Timothy 3;14-17; I Peter 3:15.

# 1 Why Is There Suffering In The World?

"Why *is* there suffering in the world?" Actually, the question usually assumes a more personal, even paranoid, tone: "Why am *I* being made to suffer like this?" We seldom volunteer for misery; it's inflicted on us. And, our aching self reasons, where there's infliction there must be an Inflictor. The aloof philosopher may ponder the abstract issue of suffering in the world, but as far as we're concerned, there's nothing abstract or philosophical about it! We hurt and we want to know, "Why is God doing this to me?"

If we were Buddhists, perhaps, the answer would be simpler. We would believe that existence and suffering are one; therefore our only escape from suffering would be to get out of existence itself. We would faithfully repeat our creed: *Ameisa, Dukka, Annath.* "Impermanence, Suffering, Emptiness."

Buddhism's passive resignation to fate is not, for most

of us, a very satisfying way to deal with pain. We identify more with the spunky style of the Jews, whose racial history is a chronicle of suffering. Out of their collective anguish has come a host of humorous anecdotes, proof of their spirit. From Communist Russia came this well-traveled story. A Russian Jew goes to see God to ask, "Is it true that you are *our* God?"

"Yes, my son," God answers.

"And is it true that we are your Chosen People?"

"Yes, my son."

"Well . . . couldn't you choose somebody else for awhile?"[1] The biblical record testifies that being God's Chosen People is no protection against every kind of human adversity.

The Buddhist seeks to escape suffering by fleeing existence. The Jew faces up to its inevitability and seeks relief in laughter. What are Christians to do?

They are to do exactly what we are doing now. They are first, to seek a better understanding of the source of suffering, and secondly, to turn their negative experiences into spiritual profit.

First, then, we raise again the fundamental question: Why do people suffer?

The most sensible answer I have studied is found in the opening pages of Genesis. In the beginning everything was fine. God made the heavens and the earth and everything in them, and it was good! God did not program suffering into his creation, but sin crept into human experience. Then the consequences.

As Genesis explains our plight, at first goodness characterized the highest form of God's creativity, male and female *homo sapiens*, born whole, born of the love of God. A glorious creation they were, innocent, attractive, comfortable, and free . . . free to love, and free to rebel.

Their rebellion against God's will altered the Creator's original design. "Creation was subjected to frustration . . ." (Rom. 8:20). Our no longer innocent parents experienced alienation — from each other, from God, from their environment. They were suddenly revealed to themselves, seeing what they had never seen before and feeling what they had never felt: fear. Now they who had enjoyed communion with God dreaded His appearing. Dismayed by their defiance, God dismissed them from what our current slang would call their "comfort zone." Their former easy relationship with the earth was no more; now they had to do combat with it as against a resisting antagonist. From its unwilling grasp they had to wrest their daily bread.

> Cursed is the ground because of you; through painful toil you will eat of it all the days of your life. It will produce thorns and thistles for you, and you will eat the plants of the field. By the sweat of your brow you will eat your food . . . (Gen. 3:17-19).

Genesis does not allow us to explain suffering away with a flip, "God did this to me," or with a belief in some starcrossed destiny before which we are helpless pawns.

> The fault, dear Brutus, is not in our stars, but in ourselves. . . .[2]

## But Where Does My Suffering Come From?

The Genesis solution to our inquiry may be correct in general, but it hardly appeases our longing to understand why we, personally, can't escape. Granted that from Adam and Eve their descendents have been victims of affliction. Why can't we avoid it? More pertinently, why can't I? What does that original rebellion have to do with my pain? I'm not a rebel, at least not any more. I'm serving God with all my heart, doing my best to be my best for His sake. Surely God could prevent my anguish if He would. Where does this suffering come from?

It has many sources, but they can be summarized in two categories: natural and human. *It's natural.* Insurance companies and lawyers use the regrettable term "Acts of God" for eruptions in nature that take their human toll. The language is unfair to God, but it does serve to remind us that some things are simply beyond our control. Floods, hurricanes, tornadoes, earthquakes, forest fires, famine and other natural phenomena render us impotent. Even people who don't believe in God speak of God acting in these events, though God would undoubtedly prefer we not give Him the undeserved blame.

These outbursts of "unfinished creation"[3] seem even worse to us if we believe physical death is the worst of all evils, a strange but not uncommon view for a Christian to hold. (We are anything but consistent, aren't we, since we also believe heaven offers a far better life than earth can afford. Why should we grieve when a loved one leaves earth for heaven?).

We compound our distress by quantitative thinking. Somehow, we have decided, when a plane crashes and kills 260 or a war breaks out and kills tens of thousands, the suffering is worse than when one pedestrian is hit by a car and dies.

When we trace suffering not only to so-called (and misnamed) "Acts of God" but also to our twisted, quantified notions of human worth, we have correctly identified one of its sources. Even in these brief paragraphs, however, we have blurred the line between natural and human causes. Is a plane crash an "Act of God" or the result of human manufacturing or piloting error? Is it to be blamed on God? Even famine could be blamed on drought — or on governmental mismanagement of distribution.

*It's self imposed.* Usually overlooked in any discussion of this subject is the truth that much of our pain is self-inflicted, often through sheer *folly*. Life-long tobacco smokers have run a high risk of incurring cancer. Excessive drinkers who drive can't blame nature or God for their accidents. All persons who indulge negative attitudes and emotions are steadily poisoning their bodies and their relationships. Dedicated athletes may think they are exercising discipline and self-control as they batter their bodies about, but they are predestining their bodies to a pain-filled post-playing-days existence.

Is there a worse offender than football? At our near-by Arizona State University, the brutal game was born in 1896 (long before the little school had grown into a university). Fred "Cap" Irish was the founder of the sport. He enrolled sixty-one male students, none of whom had ever played the game. Cap's teams preferred the old flying wedge strategy, although strategy may be too inflated a term for the chaotic colliding of bodies masquerading as organized competition. In those days players wore no helmets or shoulder pads. Substitutions were not made for strategic purposes, but only because one of the on-field players was too groggy to stand up any longer. The only mercy shown was in preparing for the game: somebody plowed the field to cushion the falls.[4]

We can't blame God for the price these young men later paid in their stove-up maturity. Nor can we blame

God for consequences of the many other diverse and amazingly inventive follies we have pursued.

There's a more favorable word to be spoken about self-inflicted suffering, however. It is often the welcomed consequence of *love*. There is no other adequate explanation, for example, of Jesus' crucifixion.

"From that time on Jesus began to explain to his disciples that he must go to Jerusalem and suffer. . . . (Matt. 16:21).

He suffered, we are told, because He loved. We call his final days of ministry, including his betrayal, trial, and execution, the Passion Week, from a word signifying both intense feeling and love.

Ask the mother of a desperately sick child why she is depriving herself of food and company and sleep to take care of the little one? Who hurts more, the mother or the child? Why does she tolerate it? Why doesn't she forget the child and take care of her own feelings? The question is absurd, isn't it, if you know anything at all about love.

> Greater love has no one than this, that one lay down his life for his friends [or children, or parents, or loved one, or country or . . . ] (John 15:13).

> [Love] always protects, always trusts, always hopes, always perseveres. Love never fails (I Cor. 13:7-8).

Noted German theologian Dietrich Bonhoeffer, safe in America away from Hitler's Nazis, made the fateful decision to return to his homeland to oppose the Reich Chancellor, even though he knew he was facing certain persecution. He believed, however, that if he refused to go through the trials of his people before Hitler's defeat, he would be unfit to participate "in the reconstruction of

Christian life in Germany after the war." The choice before his fellow believers was terrible.

> Christians in Germany will face the terrible alternative of either willing the defeat of their nation in order that Christian civilization may survive, or willing the victory of their nation and thereby destroying our civilization. I know which of these alternatives I must choose; but I cannot make this choice in security.

So he returned and was quickly arrested, the Gestapo incarcerating him on April 5, 1943. While he was in prison, he amazed his fellow inmates by asking for permission to minister to the sick and anxious and depressed. Just before the Germans surrendered, he was shot and killed.[5]

His bravery is perhaps less remarkable than we might imagine. Who does not have a love — for country, for cause, for a person or persons — so deep that he willingly risks himself for the sake of the one loved? If suffering be the consequence, it is with rejoicing (See Col. 1:24; I Pet. 1:6-8; 4:12-16).

## What's the Good of Suffering

So far our quest has been in the wrong direction. We have been looking at suffering's cause instead of its result. Some of the suggestions have been worth considering, but too much probing to find the definitive, all-encompassing explanation will end in frustration. It remains one of the great philosophical questions of all time. And when you have answered it, you still aren't content, because there is another, far more compelling question you must answer: What is it good for?

Here we are on surer ground. In God's economy nothing is wasted. Instead, "in all things God works for the good of those who love him, who have been called according to his purpose" (Rom. 8:28). Since He does, it behooves us to discover the good in all things, even when some of the things hurt.

*Your suffering can bring you closer to God.* At the mere mention of suffering a Bible student thinks of Job. Deprived of his sheep, his servants, his house, his sons and daughters and their families, afflicted by boils and tormented by his wife and friends, the besieged man still refuses to desert God. "Though he slay me, yet will I hope in him," he avows.[6] From chapter three through chapter 37, Job and his friends explore the theme of suffering. The drama, in fact, is practically devoid of action; it's all talk. Our attention is riveted on the discussion, the search for some reason for Job's inexplicable fall from prosperity. Why was he who had so much reduced to so little?

Job's plight defies conventional wisdom. How could a just God, loving and powerful, have so arbitrarily brought about his downfall? Job and his friends were not privy to the wager between God and Satan in chapters 1 and 2. They could not know that Job suffers precisely *because* he is pleasing to God and not otherwise. God believes in him; He thinks Satan cannot corrupt His man Job, so He allows the devilish testing. Job's friends, ignorant of the cosmic bet, are therefore forced to conclude, on the basis of all they know about God's righteousness and justice, that Job must have been punished for some unconfessed sin.

Job can't accept their judgment. He knows he hasn't sinned. (God agrees. See 2:3). This suffering isn't punishment.

Whether you like the resolution of the drama or not,

with God refusing to honor Job's urgent request for understanding, you must admit something unforeseen happens in the course of the book. Job, still believing in God but quite put out at His treatment of him, learns once and for all that he cannot comprehend God's incomprehensible ways. But in the course of the trial, he and God draw closer to one another. Further, both prove faithful. Job passes his test: he proves his faith in God is not based on blessings, but on trust. God in the end restores Job to his former prosperity and more.

Philip Yancey, meditating on this remarkable book, comes to the conviction that, once he states it, seems the only proper reading of the book.

> I hesitate to write this, because it is a hard truth, and one I do not want to acknowledge. But Job convinces me that God is more interested in our faith than in our pleasure. [7]

This is undoubtedly why the sages of Judaism added Job to the Old Testament canon. It violates our sentimental picture of a sugar-daddy God who dispenses his favors to His pets and metes out harsh judgments against whoever displeases Him; instead, it presents God as powerful but personal, seeking a relationship, wanting us to desire Him for Himself, not merely for what we can get out of Him. He is, in spite of all we do to change Him into something more acceptable to our demands, still God.

As a matter of fact, haven't you discovered your relationship with the Lord deepening when you hurt? And haven't you found yourself forgetting Him when times are good and the living is easy?

No complaints have I heard more often in the counseling room than this one: "What have I done wrong? I must have done something wrong. Where did I go astray? Why is God punishing me?" The answer may very well be that you are suffering not because you did something wrong but because you are doing right.

Through suffering you will also *grow deeper as a person.*

> You may my glories and my state depose, But not my griefs; still am I king of those,

contended Shakespeare's King Richard II. Glories and power are external stuff; grief and heartache are deep down in, where character is formed and wisdom is learned. Feodor Dostoevsky, the great Russian novelist, spent several years in lonely exile in Siberia before emerging as one of his country's supreme authors. Having earned in banishment the right to speak on our subject, he later said somewhere that "suffering is the sole origin of human consciousness."

Robert Louis Stevenson is frequently cited on this subject because of his victorious living in spite of so much personal pain. This is his own account:

> For fourteen years I have had not a day's real health; I have wakened sick and gone to bed weary; and I have done my day unflinchingly. I have written in bed, and written out of it, written in hemorrhages, written in sickness, and for so long, it seems to me I have won my wager and recovered my love. . . . And the battle goes on — ill or well, is a trifle, so as it goes. I was made for a contest, and the Powers have so willed that my battle-field should be this dingy, inglorious one of the bed and the physic bottle.[8]

Yet in just this condition he completed some of his finest works. We can't help asking of him, or of the deaf

Beethoven or the blind Milton or the tubercular Keats, could they have done so well, probed so profoundly, taught so wisely, had they not anguished so deeply?

President Corazon Aquino of the Philippines said in a *TIME* interview that when her late husband was imprisoned the experience improved them, bringing out "a whole new set of values for both of us."

> I didn't go beyond the people I knew. I didn't reach out. Then, all of a sudden, with my husband in prison, he was suffering, I was suffering. Yet we knew that others were worse off. *We* didn't have to worry about where our next meal was coming from or whether our children could go to school. So then, I guess, I started to worry about other people. I guess I identified myself with the victims of Marcos' injustice.[9]

The writer of Hebrews insists "No discipline seems pleasant at the time, but painful. Later on, however, it produces a harvest of righteousness and peace for those who have been trained by it" (See Heb. 12:7-11, esp. 10,11). The New Testament here and everywhere promotes the disciplined life. It never promises absence of sorrow. Its goal is the complete person in Christ, fully mature; such maturity is impossible without discipline and love and commitment. Without suffering, none of these is possible. In no other way is character built.

One of the finest illustrations of this process was published in *Leadership* magazine a few years ago. Beth Landers tells the story.

> A man found a cocoon of the emperor moth and took it home to watch it emerge. One day a small opening appeared, and for several hours the moth struggled but couldn't seem to force its body past a certain point.

Deciding something was wrong, the man took scissors and snipped the remaining bit of cocoon. The moth emerged easily, its body large and swollen, the wings small and shriveled.

He expected that in a few hours the wings would spread out in their natural beauty, but they did not. Instead of developing into a creature free to fly, the moth spent its life dragging around a swollen body and shriveled wings.

The constricting cocoon and the struggle necessary to pass through the tiny opening are God's way of forcing fluid from the body into the wings. The "merciful" snip was, in reality, cruel. Sometimes the struggle is exactly what we need.[10]

Beth Landers' story is almost the perfect parable to illustrate the struggle, the pain, the overcoming of obstacles essential in forming a free, mature individual.

It's a good parable for parents, isn't it? America is well on the way to destroying a generation of children, with of course the best of intentions. We don't want our offspring to struggle the way we did. We want to protect them, to shield them from all harm, to ease their struggle. They must dress better than we dressed, live better than we lived, to have it easier than we did. So we cripple them.

It's also a good parable for self-application, isn't it? We live in a consumer society, residing and driving in air-conditioned splendor, collecting and admiring our toys. "I paid my dues," we boast, somewhat defensively. "It's time for me to say to my soul, 'Soul, take your ease, eat, drink and be merry.' " We settle down, indulge our every whim, and stop growing. Once we dedicate ourselves to the perpetuation of our own ease, we quickly slip into dis-ease. Don't ask the Lord to guard you from all discomfort; ask for strength in the struggle.

E. Stanley Jones has recorded a true story that makes the same point. An Indian lady lived as an invalid because of an affliction of the spine. She got around on crutches, but one day she fell on the steps, breaking one crutch and losing the other as she fell. She called for help, but no one was around to help her. Finally, praying, she drew herself up by the banister, struggled to her feet, and to her surprise, walked. She never used her crutches again. "The best thing that ever happened to her was that fall," Dr. Jones writes, "though for the moment it seemed calamity on calamity. But out of the cloud came the Voice that said, 'Rise up and walk.' "[11]

Out of adversity comes advantage, out of weakness comes strength, out of suffering, depth. Perhaps that's why there's suffering in the world.

Genesis 3:17-19

Job 1-2; 13:15; 38-42

Matthew 16:21

John 15:13

Romans 8:28

I Corinthians 13:7-8

Hebrews 12:7-11

**Endnotes**

**1.** I most recently came across this story in Mark Ya. Azbel's account of his life as a Jew persecuted for his faith in the Soviet Union, *Refusenick*. London: Hamish Hamilton Pub., co. 1981, p.17.

**2.** Shakespeare, *Julius Caesar, I,* i. 139, 140.

**3.** See Romans 8:19-22. Paul teaches that creation itself looks forward to its release from bondage to decay and frustration.

**4.** From Marshall Trimble, *Roadside History of Arizona.* Missoula: Mountain Press Pub. Co., co. 1986, p. 194.

**5.** Dietrich Bonhoeffer, *The Cost of Discipleship*. New York: Macmillan Publishing Company, co. 1937, p. 16,17.

**6.** Job 13:15. See also 9:33 and 16:19-21. Job isn't entirely pleased with the way God seems to be treating him.

**7.** "When the Facts Don't Add Up," *Christianity Today*, June 13, 1986, p. 22.

**8.** Quoted in Ralph W. Sockman, *The Meaning of Suffering*. New York, Nashville: Abingdon Press, co. 1961, pp. 82-83.

**9.** January 5, 1987, p. 33.

**10.** "Struggle," *Leadership*, Fall 1984, p. 47.

**11.** *Christ and Human Suffering*. Nashville: Abingdon Press, co. 1933, p. 204.

# 2

# Will There Ever Be A Cure For All Diseases?

"Will there ever be a cure for all *my* diseases?" Yes, but you will have to die first. The New Testament promises a new heaven and earth in the life beyond this one; there God "will wipe every tear from [your] eyes. There will be no more death or mourning or crying or pain, for the old order of things [will have] passed away" (Rev. 21:4). This side of heaven, though, the old order prevails, in spite of our best efforts to overturn it.

Some of our efforts, although futile, have the touch of grandeur about them. In the years 735-37 A.D., a smallpox epidemic decimated the imperial court of Japan. To avoid a recurrence of that plague in 749, Empress Koken ordered a special corps of 116 priests to drive out the disease demons. She remembered an incident from her study of Buddhist scriptures. A sick Brahmin had consulted a seer who prophecied that the Brahmin was fated to die within seven days. Upon receiving the dire news, he went straight to the Buddha himself and offered himself as a disciple in exchange for a cure.

Buddha instructed him to go to a certain city where a pagoda had fallen. He was to repair it and then place in it a charm he would write. If he would obey, the charm would lengthen his life here and guarantee his entry into Paradise later.

Buddha's other disciples asked the source of the charm's power. He said, "Whoever wishes to gain power from the *dharani* [charm] must write seventy-seven copies and place them in a pagoda. This pagoda must then be honored with sacrifice. But one can also make seventy-seven pagodas of clay to hold the *dharani* and place one in each. This will save the life of him who thus makes and honors the pagodas, and his sins will be forgiven. Such is the method of the use of the *dharani*. . . ."

If seventy-seven were good enough for the Brahmin, the Empress Koken believed, a million charms would do the trick for her empire. That's how many charms she ordered, each a single sheet bearing about twenty-five lines of printed text in a tiny wooden pagoda. Twenty-one years later the task was finished; the million pagodas (most of them three-storied, about four and a half inches high and three and a half inches in diameter at the base) were distributed among the country's various temples. For good measure, one in 10,000 pagodas was seven-storied, and one in 100,000 thirteen-storied. The enclosed charms were the earliest examples of copper block printing on paper.

As I said, it was a grand effort. It was an enormous effort to do away with just one disease. But the *dharani* didn't work. The Empress died at the age of fifty-two, probably of smallpox, the very year the project was completed.[1]

Smallpox is no longer a threat, but into its dreaded place have stepped new and more exotic ones: Legionnaires Disease, AIDS, Alzheimer's, to name a few.

Will there ever be a cure for all diseases?

No, and yes. No, because sin and death are the natural order of things on earth. Yes, because this order isn't God's final creation.

It's fascinating, isn't it, that Jesus didn't propose a panacea nor attempt to wipe disease off even his portion of the face of the earth. He never promised His disciples protection against the ravages of disease. He cured sick people, many of them, but He didn't destroy disease. He healed personally, and He empowered His disciples to heal, but always on an individual basis. He didn't banish germs or viruses to another universe.

What would a disease-free, deathless life be like? We're not the first ones to ask the question. It's been probed by many of the world's greatest thinkers. In Homer's *Odyssey*, for example, Odysseus meets Calypso, a sea princess and a child of immortal gods. Like them, Calypso will live forever. She doesn't think the prospect's so wonderful, however. When she meets Odysseus, she is fascinated by him, having never been in the society of mortals before. Surprisingly, it is she who envies him. Living with the certainty of death enhances life's meaning, deepens its significance, she believes. Every choice takes on heightened importance. Apparently the wise Homer would not have us escape all disease or death.

Jonathan Swift takes a slightly different approach with his Luggnaggians in *Gulliver's Travels.* Once or twice in every generation a Luggnaggian child was born with a red circular spot on its forehead; one so favored would never die. Gulliver is envious at first, until he observes how miserable they are. Though immortal, they still grow old and feeble, outliving their friends and contemporaries. When they turn eighty, their property is legally taken from them and given to their children. Their bodies contract various ailments, their psyches accumulate grudges and bitterness, they grow tired of the struggle of life — and they can never anticipate any release.

The Luggnaggians, immortal but not immune to disease, face a bleak future. Homer's Calypso, immortal *and* immune to disease, nevertheless envies the limited existence of mortal, sickness-prone man. Perhaps a total escape from disease is not really to be desired.

## Many Remedies Have Been Proposed

You'd never know it, though, from the nostrums that wizards, witch doctors, apothecaries, charlatans and even well-meaning medical persons have foisted on a gullible public. In my own state, a fascinating conglomeration of remedies has been peddled to cure everything from anemia to zits. Territorial Arizona was short on chemicals but long on creativity. No self-respecting householder would have been without calomel, turpentine, laudanum (tincture of opium), castor oil, paregoric, and Seidlitz powders.

Those were the standards but seem rather unimaginative when compared with . . .

— Cow manure for treating foot rash, packing wounds, and as a poultice for pneumonia

— Cowboy urine for rope burns

— Eating an apple after driving several iron nails into it and leaving them overnight, for anemia. (Of course, you extracted the nails before biting the apple.)

— Drinking tea made from cockroaches for lockjaw
— Eating round beetles as a more generalized cure
— For warts, "wet the hand, pour salt over it, and let a horse kick it. At least the specific problem of warts was forgotten by following this rather dubious remedy."[2]

In the Wild West as in our days, religions offered the ultimate power for conquering disease. Christian Science's Mary Baker Eddy, when she was still Mrs. Glover, inserted this advertisement in *THE BANNER OF LIGHT* for July 4, 1869:

> Any person desiring to learn how to heal the sick can receive of the undersigned instruction that will enable them to commence healing on a principle of science with success far beyond any of the present modes. No medicine, electricity, physiology or hygiene required for unparalleled success in the most difficult cases. No pay required unless the skill is obtained. . . .

That Mrs. Eddy has many spiritual descendants proclaiming their miraculous powers today needs no documentation. Why, one wonders, hasn't disease been eliminated, since Mrs. Eddy promised to teach anyone to heal the sick. By now we should have all healed each other!

My piano teacher's husband was a member of Mrs. Eddy's religion. He was devoted to Christian Science, insisting that illness was a state of mind and did not really exist. One day my piano teacher's husband became sick and died.

A new twist to this old theme has been the rise of a new breed of religionists called the New Age-ers. While rejecting organized religion's claims, they make some pretty fantastic ones of their own. They don't talk of faith-healing or Christian science or incredible elixirs like

Geritol. They are, for example, more into "crystal consciousness," the pseudoscientific belief that natural gemstones like quartz crystal, citrine, tourmaline, and amethyst have paranormal healing and restorative powers. They may be modern, these New-Agers, but *Time* reports,

> . . . age-old rite and techno-trend vocabulary meet in "programming" or getting the most out of your talisman. One West Coast formula for doing so goes this way: first, "clear" the stone by washing it in ocean water (in a pinch, salt water will do). Then leave it outside for at least 24 hours so that rays of the sun and moon may penetrate it. A quicker, high-tech method is to pass an audiocassette eraser over each side of the crystal for half a minute. To program, after the crystal has been cleared, hold it in both hands and blow on it while making a wish. For good health, for instance, one might say, "I want this energy to aid my immune system." Or you . . . hold the stone over your solar plexus for two minutes and repeat, "This blue topaz is vibrating to calm my nervous system."[3]

So the beat goes on. From earliest history we have sought cures for every conceivable illness and have dreamed of a Fountain of Youth or a magical potion that would once and for all (or even for a time) banish all disease. None has been found, in spite of the ingenuity of their advertisers. Even New-Agers get sick and die.

### No Cure-all So Long As We Have Human Freedom

The fact to be faced, as we noted in the last chapter, is that like suffering, disease will not be banished so long as nature is nature and human beings are human beings. We demand the right to harm ourselves.

Thanks to the discoveries of modern medical science, however, we've made enormous progress in treating illnesses in the last century. In fact, in mid-nineteenth century, "conditions were so bad that at University College Hospital, London, a death rate of 25 percent was considered satisfactory compared with rates of 39 percent in Glasgow, 43 percent in Edinburgh, and a staggering 59 percent in Paris."[4] You obviously didn't want to get sick. If you did, the last place you wanted to go was the hospital! The greatest killer in hospitals was infectious disease — with the infections being blithely transferred by unwashed medical attendants.

Yes, we've come a long way, but with progress has come a new danger: unrealistic expectations. We have transferred our faith in God to faith in doctors. When they don't cure us as we demand, we sue for malpractice. We shop doctors until we find one who will tell us what we want to hear. We can't quite believe there's no quick and easy fix for our aches and pains. And we refuse to accept any explanation that links lifestyle to lumbago.

Norman Cousins insists that "the most costly disease in America is not cancer or coronaries," but boredom. Pain, he insists, is most frequently the result of,

> . . . tensions, stress, worry, idleness, boredom, frustration, suppressed rage, insufficient sleep, overeating, a poorly balanced diet, smoking, excessive drinking, inadequate exercise, stale air, or any of the other abuses encountered by the human body in modern society.[5]

Cousins criticizes us for grabbing instinctively for painkillers instead of eliminating the abuse we heap on our bodies. (He also notes that "most men think they are immortal — until they get a cold, then they think they are going to die within the hour." We can tolerate anything except discomfort.)

## What About You And Me?

Let's become personal now. While you and I will undoubtedly agree it's fruitless to hope for the end of all illness this side of heaven, we have every right to believe our Lord is as interested in our good health today as He was when He touched and made people whole during His earthly ministry.

Fully trusting this is so, let me make the following suggestions based on the Bible's teachings.

*Be as healthy as you can.* Several of my medical friends have said their greatest frustration is with patients who refuse to come to them until it's almost too late. They cheerfully ignore and abuse their bodies until, their nerves screaming in pain, they rush to the doctor yelling "emergency" and expect him to perform a miracle.

Some doctor friends have even wished longingly for my job. A psychiatrist says ministers can do more to make people well than a psychiatrist can. He can help them in his consulting office, he said, and prescribe some pills, but he then has to release them to the same home and environment that promoted their sickness in the first place. The minister, on the other hand, introduces them into a healing community where the good he does them in the office is furthered in their new friends and supporters. Furthermore, the church helps people practice preventive medicine through education programs and visitation and training in building healthy relationships. The typical physician is always trying to cure, playing catch-up.

Every survey on the subject I have ever read has confirmed that church-going people are healthier than the general population. To be as healthy as you can be, then, means participating in the life of the church, studying

God's word, living a Christian lifestyle, praying and praising.[6]

*Learn from others' examples.* Let me give you the advice a dying man asked me to pass on to you. Having become a Christian in mid-life, this life-long cigarette smoker quit just a few years before his death. He was now paying for his habit with terminal lung cancer. Every breath painful, he begged me to warn everybody I could. "Use me as an example," he said. "Let them know the consequences of smoking." So I am warning you. Learn from another's example.

Our ability to deceive ourselves is quite extraordinary. Somehow we believe that, no matter what we do, we'll escape the consequences of our choices. We know the Bible says, "Do not be deceived: God cannot be mocked. A man reaps what he sows" (Gal. 6:7). We hear, but we don't always heed.

There's a marvelous line in Peter's sermon in the third chapter of Acts.

> Repent, then, and turn to God, so that your sins may be wiped out, that times of refreshing may come from the Lord. (Acts 3:19).

When you have repented, when you turn your life Godward, when the company you keep is also seeking the Lord, your good, clean, wholesome life will result in improved health. You will be renewed and *refreshed*, like springtime and youth all over again.

Wise is the person who learns from others. Steady use of tobacco does lead to cancer and heart disease. Abuse of chemical substances does destroy health and home and happiness. Storing up anger and bitterness does cripple souls and bodies.

Just look around. The examples are everywhere.

*Beware of quacks — religious or medical.* When your body is hurting, you're easy to con. For a quick profit, certain people in every profession will promise you what they can't deliver. What horror stories we hear of people who have emptied their savings and exhaused themselves in vain pursuit of bogus promises. I thank God daily for the legitimate practitioners of the healing arts; I'm a fan of good physicians. (As a youth I had thought for awhile of going into medicine, before becoming convinced of my call into the ministry.) Among my friends are several outstanding physicians whose ethics, character, and professional competence I admire. I'm not warning you to beware the likes of these. Remember, though: the good ones don't make promises they can't keep. They don't play God; they serve Him.

You must also be aware by now that I am a minister who is proud of his calling. Among the most outstanding persons I know are some holy, conscientious, learned pastors. I'm not warning you to beware the likes of them, either. Like physicians, however, the good ones don't play God either; they serve Him.

But both the medical and the religious professions are bedevilled (the appropriate word) by humbugs and hucksters whose concern is their belly, not your betterment. They know what TV executives know: we are suckers for white gowns, white collars, and white lies. We so much want to believe in someone else's infallibility that we gladly place our destinies in their hands, if only they sound authoritative and flash their credentials. Beware the likes of them.

An intriguing study published by John and Sonja McKinlay of Boston University in 1977 concludes that, all other things being equal, the *fewer* doctors there are in a population the *lower* the mortality rate. In addition, and equally intriguing, is their discovery that whenever there is a doctors' strike — as there have been in recent years in the U.S., Canada, England, and Israel — the death rates in the affected areas actually *fall*. It seems when people must, they take charge of their own physical health — and it improves!

Beware the glittering reputations of television celebrities, too, even your favorite religious entertainers. Television is a fabulous medium, seemingly able to transform very ordinary men and women into paragons of piety and power. The scandals that rocked the televangelism empire in the late 1980s should have taught us all not to throw our money at the feet of Big Names, even religious ones.

I need to assure you that I've seen healing; I have even participated in healing ministries. They weren't on television, though. I'm not saying that all televised healing services are hokum, but I do have my doubts. Do you remember when the Devil was tempting Jesus? Satan said, "I'll take you up to the pinnacle of the temple and I will throw you down . . ." (Matt. 4:1-11). Think of how the publicity would have helped Jesus' career, to be thrown from the temple and have the angels come and catch Him. He refused. By turning his back on Satan at that moment, He conquered the temptation to bedazzle the masses, to attract great attention to Himself. Similarly, throughout His ministry it is apparent that when Jesus touched someone, what He was after was healing, not hype.

What I am suggesting is that you and I would be better off relying first of all on our own resources (and God's), rather than on any human miracle-worker. When we need help, though, we must seek out the most competent, not merely the most celebrated.

Finally, *seek the full will of God.* There's no doubt about it: God wants us whole. John's prayer is for all God's people:

> Dear friend, I pray that you may enjoy good health and that all may go well with you, even as your soul is getting along well (III John 2).

Note how deftly John interweaves our soul's wellbeing, our generally positive circumstances, and our good physical health. It's fair to assume God wants us to have it all. Earlier we looked at James' teaching on the subject, in which he virtually promises health through the prayers of the elders. In addition, James ties together the forgiveness of sins and the return of good health:

> If he has sinned, he will be forgiven (James 5:15).

Hence the importance of confession of sins and prayer for one another. Hence also the importance of mutuality in the healing process and of confessing, that is, opening up and purging oneself of the poison of sin and guilt. So

> pray for each other so that you may be healed. The prayer of a righteous man is powerful and effective (James 5:16).

We have come to the end of the matter. Is there a cure-all for disease? Is there some magical formula that will remove all illness? No. Your body is going to wear out. Even as I write these words some parts of my body are making certain I'm aware of their existence. They hurt. I suspect some of yours do, too. So don't be misled by religious or medical hucksters who promises you a quick cure for all sickness and physical death.

On the other hand, don't worry. Your faith in the Lord is not in vain. It is impossible for you to conform yourself to the will of God and walk with Him daily without your body feeling the difference.

As for me, when I was an asthmatic child I never expected to be a healthy adult. As an adult, however, I have lived a more vigorous life than I ever dreamed was possible. What happened? I sought good health, of course, following the best medical advice I could find. More than that, though, I decided to serve the Lord with whatever health I had. I took seriously Jesus' promise that those who sought first "His kingdom and His righteousness," could expect Him to take care of the rest (Matt. 6:33). He has.

What has been true for me can be true for you, also.

Proverbs 17:22
Matthew 4:1-11; 6:25-33
Acts 3:19
III John 2
James 5:13-16
Revelation 21:4

**Endnotes**

1. Daniel J. Boorstin, *The Discoverers*. New York: Random House (Vintage Books), co. 1983, pp. 499-500.

2. Marshall Trimble, *Arizona*. New York: Doubleday and Company, co. 1977, pp. 300-301.

3. January 19, 1987, p. 66.

4. James Burke, *The Day the Universe Changed*. Boston, Toronto: Little, Brown and Company, co. 1985, p. 220.

**5.** *Human Options.* New York and London: W.W. Norton and Company, co. 1981, p. 216

**6.** James 5:13-16 gives more specific counsel on how to be as healthy as you can.

# 3

# Why Is There Evil In The World?

"The church has lied to us." The frustrated widow and mother of seven children lived in a modest but clean Chicago apartment. She was a survivor, having her life pretty much under control, but it wasn't easy for her. Findley Edge was interviewing her because of her participation in a church that had become rather famous for its concern about social problems. He and the lady had been exploring the subject awhile when she exploded in indignation, accusing the church of lying.

Surprised, Edge asked for more. "Well," she said, "the church told us that our problem was poor housing . . . lack of education and of inadequate wages . . . No. Our basic problem is within us. The other problems can be solved. We can get better housing, education, and wages, but this would not remedy our condition because our basic problem would still be in us. The church hasn't told us this! And that's why I say the church has lied to us."[1]

There has been a great deal of lying on this subject. No one really wants to face the truth. Why is there evil in the world? The lady is right: The problem is within us. *We* are the reason there's evil in the world.

The apostle Paul deals with this universal question in the first chapter of Romans. It's a hard hitting passage that begins with verse 18:

> The wrath of God is being revealed from heaven against all the godlessness and wickedness of men who suppress the truth by their wickedness, since what may be known about God is plain to them, because God has made it plain to them. For since the creation of the world God's invisible qualities — his eternal power and divine nature — have been clearly seen, being understood from what has been made, so that men are without excuse. For although they knew God, they neither glorified him as God nor gave thanks to him, but their thinking became futile and their foolish hearts were darkened. Although they claimed to be wise, they became fools and exchanged the glory of the immortal God for images made to look like mortal man and birds and animals and reptiles. Therefore God gave them over in the sinful desires of their hearts to sexual impurity for the degrading of their bodies with one another. They exchanged the truth of God for a lie, and worshiped and served created things rather than the Creator — who is forever praised. Amen.

Pretty clear where the responsibility lies, isn't it? Paul zeroes right in on the problem. He would agree with Pogo's famous comic strip comment: "We has seen the enemy, and he is us."

### What Is It?

Evil can be simply defined as the result of making a god or

gods of man and his works. Its companions are pride, selfishness, and godlessness.

Paul's argument is logical. First, he affirms, *God is obvious* (19-20). God has made His character ("eternal power and divine nature") plainly evident in His creation. If we do not believe or acknowledge Him, the fault is with us, not with Him. (And now, of course, we can know about Him also through Jesus Christ, who has revealed all of God that we can understand; so we are completely without excuse.)

God's power and divinity are apparent, Paul affirms. What isn't so obvious is our own nature. It isn't immediately apparent because we have done all we can to camouflage or deny it. We don't want to fully admit our capacity for both marvelous good and terrible evil. In our ability to choose lies our power to do evil.

Earlier in my life I was convinced that humanity is basically good. I suspect I picked the idea up from the easy consciences of my contemporaries. If everybody is basically good, then it follows that the practice of good is the norm and the practice of sin is an exception. Intrinsically good people, then, are the majority, and "sinners" are the minority. So I reasoned. Further, I would have been horrified had anybody suggested to me that there was such a thing as an evil person. They sinned, of course, and committed crimes, but they were not "by nature" evil. Now I know better. The truth is, if somebody decides to sin against God and other people, and then to sin again, and to sin again until the sin becomes habitual, the recurring sins form character, an evil character.

There are some people in whose presence we feel unaccountably ill at ease. I confess to being afraid of them. They seem to have turned their backs on God. Instinctively, we don't trust them. They find stretching the truth too easy. They are always looking out for themselves, without caring about anyone else. They may even use God-language, but too glibly, too selfishly. Dr. Scott Peck calls people who have given themselves over to evil *The People of the Lie*. He's convinced there is a mental health category that psychiatrists have shunned, but which is essential to understanding certain cases. He calls that category *evil*. Its primary attribute is lying. Evil people choose to lie.

The line between good and evil runs through the heart. In the struggle between right and wrong, one side or the other of our hearts prevails. Unfortunately for us, we can't just decide once for all and have it done with. Daily we must choose anew; our everyday options call for choices that reveal (and mold) our characters. Few of us always choose good or always choose evil; some of the options are trials. Like Paul, "what [we] want to do [we] do not do," and "the evil [we] do not want to do — this [we] keep on doing" (Rom. 7:14-25).

Evidence of our poor choices lies all around us. We like to boast, for example, about the goodness and greatness of our country, yet isn't it disturbing that in this age of evangelical revival, this age in which being "born again" has been such a popular claim, we are witnessing an explosion of evil? Reo M. Christenson, a political science university professor, has reflected on the absence of conservative moral and political values in the entertainment industry, for instance. Citing rock lyrics, X-rated movies and video tapes and "virtually pornographic network TV," he writes:

> Part of us is attracted by The Good; another part is attracted by scenes of violence, of illicit sex, of evil in various

> forms. A part of us wants the man on the ledge to jump. The entertainment industry exploits this dark side of our nature, cynically declares it is giving us what we want, and washes its hands of moral responsibility. It's a cheap act.[2]

Dr. Laurence J. Peter has said it well: "The reason that the way of the transgressor is so hard is because it's so crowded."[3] The entertainment industry would not provide its daily fare of exploited darkness if the crowd didn't clamor for it.

*God has been rejected and replaced.* Paul says, "The wrath of God is being revealed from heaven against all the godlessness and wickedness of men *who suppress the truth by their wickedness.*" We have chosen to dismiss God and stifle the truth.

Dr. Scott Peck, who has done some of the finest thinking about evil I have read anywhere, applauds Erich Fromm's belief that the genesis of human evil is a developmental process in which we become evil slowly over a long period of time because of the many wrong choices we make. Peck demurs somewhat, though, feeling Fromm doesn't go far enough; he underestimates the power of the will itself.

> I have seen cases in which an individual made an evil choice for no apparent reason other than the pure desire to exercise the freedom of his or her will. It is as if such people say to themselves, 'I know what is supposed to be the right action in this situation, but I am damned if I am going to be bound to notions of morality or even to my own conscience. Were I to do the good thing, it would be because it is good. But if I do the bad thing, it will be solely because I want to. Therefore I shall do the bad, because it is my freedom to do so.'[4]

Such persons sound like Adam and Eve, don't they?

Because they were free to choose the wrong, they chose it. No other justifiable reason. Their descendents picked up the practice after them. Read the first several stories of Genesis. You'll detect a pattern there. Whenever men receive new knowledge or skill or pleasure, they first make selfish use of it, to their own detriment. Adam and Eve, Cain and Abel, Noah and the Flood, and the Tower of Babel — the stories have the same moral. From our original parents' decision to deny God's authority over them to the series climax, with Babel's newly-skilled builders challenging the domain of God and bringing ruin upon themselves, (Gen. 11:1-9) the outcome is the same. Wrong choices lead to disaster.

> For although they knew God, they neither glorified him as God nor gave thanks to him, but their thinking became futile and their foolish hearts were darkened. Although they claimed to be wise, they became fools and exchanged the glory of the immortal God for images made to look like mortal man and birds and animals and reptiles (Rom. 1:21-23).

So they — and we — have chosen, have deliberately voted to worship a substitute, lest we give the wrong impression. We don't want anything to think we have actually submitted to God.

So what option is left for Him? *God has had to abandon them.*

> Therefore, God gave them over in the sinful desires of their hearts to sexual impurity for the degrading of their bodies with one another (Rom. 1:24).

As we have already noted, the scriptures make one thing perfectly clear. God lets us decide, and He will not override our decision. God will allow us to go to hell, if we so desire. He will, if we reject Him, reluctantly, heart-brokenly, but finally, abandon us to our appetities.

> Because of this, God gave them over to shameful lusts. Even their women exchanged natural relations for unnatural ones (Rom. 1:26).

If we prefer depravation to holiness, we can have it.

> Furthermore, since they did not think it worthwhile to retain the knowledge of God, he gave them over to a depraved mind, to do what ought not to be done. They have become filled with every kind of
> wickedness
> evil
> greed and depravity.
> They are full of
> envy
> murder
> strife
> deceit and malice.
> They are gossips
> slanderers
> God-haters
> insolent
> arrogant and boastful;
> they invent ways of doing evil . . . (Rom. 1:28-30).

On and on it goes, worse and worse it gets. Where did it begin? It began when they chose to turn their back on God.

### What Shall We Do About It?

It's not enough just to say there is evil. It's not enough

to sympathize with the victims of evil persons. What are we going to do about it?

*One possible — but wrong-headed — solution.* The English nation proposed a radical resolution to the whole problem a couple of centuries ago. In 1787 the British government sent a fleet of prisoners to colonize far-away Australia. As far as English leadership was concerned, evil was a class problem. At the bottom of society was the criminal class; England could only be purified by exporting all members of that criminal class to a far off penal colony. Australia was the continent of choice. Thanks to their wrongheaded policy, we have all the proof we need that evil is not the exclusive property of any group of people. Something interesting happened down under. Some of those criminals turned out to be sterling citizens, while at the same time back in the homeland criminal behavior flourished as bountifully as ever. Evil doesn't run in classes, but through human hearts in every caste.

*God's far different solution to the problem.* He solved it by way of a cross. Understanding the potential for criminality in us all ("All have sinned and fall short of the glory of God," Rom. 3:23), and having established the inexorable law of consequence ("the wages of sin is death," Rom. 6:23), God moved to rescue us from ourselves.

I still find the Gospel story almost incredible. He who looked deep into our blackened and divided hearts did not abandon us nor did He ship us off to some far away continent, but instead, He sent His Son at just the right time, when we were still powerless, to rescue the ungodly by way of a cross (Rom. 5:6-8).

When Mahatma Ghandi was assassinated, somebody said, "This shows how dangerous it is to be good." That lesson had already been taught by Jesus' death. It was dangerous for Him to come, deadly for Him to be so good. He paid the price so that we might be rescued.

Rescued from what? From the clutches of Satan? That's one way to put it. But another way to state it brings the truth closer to home and forces us to face up to something we would rather deny. He came to save us from ourselves, from our propensity to make the wrong decisions. To pick the wrong choice.

He came to save us from that duplicity that lies within us and causes us to lie.

*A Christian's response.* French writer Andre Malraux once asked a priest, "How long have you been hearing confessions?"

The priest said, "Fifteen years."

"What has confession taught you about men?"

The priest gave two answers. "First," he said, "people are much more unhappy than one thinks . . . and then. . . ."

"And then, the fundamental fact is that *there's no such thing as a grown-up person.*"[5]

Each of the priest's statements explains the other. There's no such thing as a grown-up person; that's why so many people are unhappy. You cannot be a chronological adult behaving like a child and be happy. You are unhappy and the cause of unhappiness. When we refuse to grow up, we contribute to the evil in this world. The Bible insists we grow up into maturity and out of selfishness. Refusal to do so is sin. Prolonged refusal to do so is evil.

Adolph Eichman illustrates the principle vividly. Remember him? In 1961, he went on trial for his leading role in the horrors of Naziism. He served Hitler as Nazi deportation and immigration czar. It was he who had the responsibility for rounding up, deporting, and annihilating Jews. Finally, long after the war was over, Israeli Nazi hunters found him hiding in his Buenos Aires, Argentina home. They dragged him back to Jerusalem for trial. During the proceedings — I remember watching it on television — he stood behind a bulletproof glass cage, with two armed guards watching every move in the courtroom. The Israelis were determined to keep him alive long enough to convict him. Charges included exterminating and sterilizing Jews, pressing them into forced labor, confiscating their property, depriving them of their livelihoods, inducing abortions in pregnant Jewish women, and stripping Jewish corpses of gold teeth and hair, artificial limbs, and clothing.

His defense was memorable. He pleaded "not guilty" on all fifteen counts. Admitting he had "regret and condemnation for the extermination of the Jewish people which was ordered by the German rulers," he completely exonerated himself. He said he could do nothing to prevent it, because he was merely "a tool in the hands of the strong and the powerful and in the hands of fate itself." The whole world heard his plea.

It was, quite simply, "I'm not responsible." It was, pitifully, the plea of immaturity. We cop this plea from earliest childhood. "I'm not responsible, I'm helpless, I can't be held accountable. I have to do what the big people tell me." Childish. And evil.

Why is there so much evil in the world? Because so many of us are like Eichman and will not act responsibly. We're like a child who, going across the room, stumbles on a chair and scolds, "Naughty chair, bad chair." Look at yourself, an adult. You're running to catch a plane, you breathlessly get in at the last moment. You sit down, the plane takes off, you discover the plane is going to a different destination from yours. What do you say? "It's the wrong plane!" (The plane's at fault, not me.) No. It's the wrong passenger!

So we proceed through life, carefully making certain whatever is wrong is somebody else's fault.

The Christian response is to face up to it, to "put childish ways behind,"(I Cor. 13:11) to be adult. Think of the child for a moment. When the baby opens his eyes he sees a world around him. The horizon of that world is defined by where he lies. Everything is defined with reference to himself. If something hurts him, he calls it bad. If something feels pleasant, he calls it good. His standard of value is totally determined by how things affect him. So, like the baby, all of us unthinkingly take our place at the center of the universe and expect everything else to fit, to exist for our pleasure. The objective fact, however, is that only God is to stand at the center of the universe; when we take His place there, the consequences for both the universe and ourselves are dire.

So long as we maintain the perspective and behavior of the baby, we're not only irresponsible and self-centered, but we are unwittingly (or deliberately) contributing to the evil that's in this world.

Pascal was right when he said, "there are only two kinds of men: The righteous who believe themselves to be sinners; the rest, sinners, who believe themselves righteous." I am afraid of the person who announces his righteousness. I'm afraid of the person who is never wrong. I'm afraid of the person who lives for himself, who manages his universe from his personal throne room. There's room for no one else there, even — especially — God.

Romans 1:18-32; 3:21-26; 5:1-8
Isaiah 47:10-11
I Corinthians 13:11
I John 3:7-10

## Endnotes

**1.** *The Greening of the Church.* Waco: Word Books, Publisher, co. 1971, p. 70.

**2.** "The Shape of Things: December 1985," *Eternity*, December 1985, p. 20.

**3.** *Peter's People.* New York: William Morrow and Company, Inc., co. 1979, p.23

**4.** *People of the Lie.* New York: Simon and Schuster (Touchstone Book), co. 1983, p. 82.

**5.** *Anti-Memoirs,* tr. by Terence Kilmartin. New York, et al: Holt, Rinehart and Winston, co. 1968, p. 1.

# 4

# Will There Ever Be Lasting World Peace?

For several years I have been leading tours to the Holy Land. Without fail, each time we prepare to leave someone worries, "Surely you're not going to go to the Holy Land now. It isn't safe! There's so much tension between the Israelis and Palestinians." My answer is always the same: "If we wait until there is no tension in the Holy Land, we'll never get to go." Throughout all history that troubled territory has been beset by wars and rumors of wars. It's easy to answer this chapter's question: Will there ever be lasting world peace? Never, so long as world peace depends on a tranquil Middle East.

Warlike conditions are our lot right up to the Lord's return:

> You will hear of wars and rumors of wars, but see to it that you are not alarmed. Such things must happen, but the end is still to come. Nation will rise against nation, and kingdom against kingdom. There will be famines and

> earthquakes in various places. All these are the beginning of birth pains (Matt. 24:6-8).

Not peace, but intensified hostilities, is Jesus' forecast. We dream with Isaiah of the day when nations

> . . . will beat their swords into plowshares
> and their spears into pruning hooks.
> Nation will not take up sword against nation,
> nor will they train for war anymore (Isaiah 2:4).

We dream on, but Jesus predicts wars and rumors of wars. In fact, the Prince of Peace shocks us still when He warns:

> Do not suppose that I have come to bring peace on earth. I did not come to bring peace, but a sword (Matt. 10:34).

> Do you think I came to bring peace on earth? No, I tell you, but division (Luke 12:51).

His goal was peace, but His effect has often been war, the inevitable result of pitting truth against falsehood, good against evil, right against wrong. We have to take care, lest, in our search for peace, we tolerate the intolerable. Neville Chamberlain returned from Munich to London in 1939, having given Hitler everything he wanted, and announced "peace in our time." His appeasing negotiations in the name of peace hastened the advent of war.

Will there ever be peace — lasting peace, or even temporary peace? We really are asking, like Chamberlain before us, can there be lasting peace in our time? The answer, offered with regret, is "No," not until the end of the world — or at least until the end of worldliness.

Let me be more specific.

*Not until man ceases to fight over national borders.*

What are our borders, anyway, but man-made inventions designed primarily to give us something to fight over? They provide a kind of perverse entertainment, so we won't grow bored with life. Is it God's design that Canadians should be distinguished from Americans by an invisible line separating them? Was it God who drew the line between Mexico and America? Why should passports be required for me to visit my friend in Poland? Or India?

Can there be peace on earth so long as people serve the needs of nations above the needs of humanity?

What Jesus did for the hostility between Jews and Gentiles He did for the divisions separating all people everywhere:

> For he himself is our peace, who has made the two one and has destroyed the barrier, the dividing wall of hostility, by abolishing in his flesh the law. . . . His purpose was to create in himself one new man out of the two, thus making peace. . . . He came and preached peace to you who were far away and peace to those who were near. For through him we both have access to the Father by one Spirit (Eph. 2:14,15,17,18)

When we are in Christ we are Christians first of all and nationals secondly. Passports aren't required to visit one another's churches all over the globe. Languages, cultures, climates may differ, but an Asian Christian, an African Christian, and an American Christian are primarily and undividedly Christian. They are at peace with one another, even when their nations are hostile.

*Not until we abandon our blind trust in military solutions to political problems.* General William Tecumseh Sherman delivered one of America's most famous speeches about war. Fourteen years following his devastating march across and through the cities of the south in the War between the States, Sherman spoke for graduation ceremonies at the Michigan Military Academy.

> War is at best barbarism. I'm tired and sick of war. Its glory is all moonshine. It is only those who have neither fired a shot nor heard the shrieks and groans of the wounded who cry aloud for blood, more vengeance, more desolation. War is hell.[1]

As close to hell as we can come on this earth, anyway. And yet, even as I'm writing this, I recall a newspaper headline: "Study: Annual world military spending reaches new high; Governments' bills total $1.8 million per minute."[2] Up to $930 billion a year the governments of this world spend for war. In this century more wars have been fought at the same time than in any other era in history. We haven't yet caught on to a most obvious fact, that you do not wage peace with war.

No, there will not be peace — lasting peace — so long as our only approach to peace is a military one. So we lament with the Psalmist:

> Too long have I lived
> among those who hate peace.
> I am a man of peace;
> but when I speak, they are for war (Psa. 120:6-7).

*Not until we worship something greater than nuclear power.*

For several decades following the dropping of the atomic bomb on Hiroshima and Nagasaki, Americans placed irrational faith in "the ultimate weapon." Even today, when world leaders are reevaluating all applications of nuclear energy because of its inherent dangers, the man in the street still believes the most powerful force in the world is nuclear power.

President Truman came close to saying the same thing. He was returing from the Potsdam Conference with Joseph Stalin and Winston Churchill aboard the steamship Augusta when the message was handed to him that the atomic bomb had fallen on Hiroshima. He face beaming, he said to the ship's pilot, "Captain, this is the greatest thing in history."[3] He later changed his assessment, but in the flush of the moment, with victory in his grasp, he said it. His fellow Americans agreed, for years. We began to think of ourselves as invincible because we had the bomb. There was no greater power.

We've been humbled since then. Now many other countries have it, and they, too, think they are somebody. I am more of the opinion of Pope John XXIII, who believed, "Nuclear war is not just a war between nations, it is a war of man against God."[4]

Whenever a nation orders a portion of the population annihilated, having decided what people have a right to live and what people ought to die, we aren't merely "playing God," we are replacing Him. It is then we who are in danger.

We should agree with the Psalmist:

> I will listen to what God the Lord will say; he promises peace to his people, his saints — but let them not return to folly (Psa. 85:8).

*Not until the world gives allegiance to God.* He alone is the source of peace. That's God, not just any god. In this essay I've been particularly critical of our allegiance to militaristic or nationalistic gods. Our blindness to this worship sometimes frightens me. Occasionally a particularly blatant symbol of such idolatry appears which should be heeded as a danger signal. It seldom is.

One appeared in New Mexico in the mid-1940's. An 18 × 24 mile strip of barren land along the San Jose Trail near Alamagordo was dedicated for the testing of the atomic bomb. Back when it was being developed, J. Robert Oppenheimer, project director, sought an appropriate name for that strip. He got the name one night when he was reading a poem by John Donne, seventeenth century British poet. It's actually a prayer, asking God to humble the poet — to beat him down if necessary — so that He can pick him up and use him.

> Batter my heart, three-personed God, for you
> As yet but knock, breathe, shine and seek to mend.
> That I may rise and stand, o'erthrow me and bend
> Your force to break, blow, burn, and make me new.

"Three-personed God," thought Oppenheimer. "That's the trinity." He had his name.[5] Trinity would "break, blow, burn," and make new. The atomic bomb would be tested on a strip of land named "Trinity." It sounds almost blasphemous to desecrate the loving God by applying one of His names to a testing ground for "the ultimate weapon." "Trinity" connotes divinity; in New Mexico, it points to a new god to worship: nuclear power.

No, there is not going to be peace on earth so long as we give our allegiance, or devotion, our worship to forces that kill instead of the Force that will make alive.

> This is the message God sent to the people of Israel, telling the good news of peace through Jesus Christ, who is Lord of all (Acts 10:36).

> Glory to God in the highest and on earth peace to men on whom his favor rests (Luke 2:14).

Peace is grounded in the holy Trinity, not the atomic one.

*Not so long as we keep on making the wrong choices.* Pilate offered to release Jesus, the peacemaker, or Barabbas, the warrior. "Give us Barabbas," crucify that other guy (Matt. 27:15-26). How foolish. How predictable. Mobs usually choose wrong.

A story made the rounds after the First World War. I can't verify its historical accuracy, but I'd like to believe it happened. In a lull in the fighting, when Germans, French and British were dug into trenches close enough to see and hear one another, over the German trenches a sign was seen flying: "The British are fools." The British quickly shot it down.

Before long another banner appeared: "The French are fools." The French shot that one down.

Then a third banner arose: "We're all fools, let's all go home."[6] This time the British response was laughter.

That would have been a wise choice — for all nations to admit their foolishness, have a good laugh, and go home. But the wise solution is seldom the popular one.

Of course, wars don't stop just because the foot soldiers want to go home. Sometimes, in fact, they don't seem stoppable. An embattled Lyndon Johnson, nearing the end of his presidency in 1964, complained to Bill Moyers, "I feel like a hitchhiker caught in a hailstorm on a Texas highway. I can't run. I can't hide. And I can't make it stop."[7] We who survived those agonizing years observed their toll on the man and on his nation. We all suffered the series of wrong choices that led to our ultimate failure in Vietnam. Competent men were guiding national policies, making "every effort to do what leads to peace and to mutual edification" (Rom. 14:19), but their sincerity wasn't enough to compensate for the bad calls.

*Not until churches shake off their indifference.* So far I've sounded pretty anti-government and anti-military. I'm neither. I'm pro-church, and I fervently believe there will be no end to war in our time until the churches of the world shake off their indifference and earnestly, sacrificially wage peace. We don't like to think about this, of course, because it places too much responsibility on us. We prefer to ask of our government, or the Russian government, or somebody's government: "Why don't *they* do something?" A strange posture, isn't it, for disciples of the Prince of Peace (Matt. 5:9)?

Oregon Senator Mark Hatfield summarizes our duties well:

> How dare we offer Christ as the Bread of Life to a hungry man when we have no compassion to find the bread to feed his stomach! I say to you, this world . . . is in need of . . . the message of redemption *and* the mission of compassion and service.[8]

When the church takes up the ministry of Jesus, offering good news to the poor, freedom for prisoners, recovery of sight for the blind, and release for the oppressed (Luke 4:18), then there is some hope that brotherhood will replace enmity. We have seen what happens when world nations try to keep the peace. We have not yet seen what can happen when the church, empowered by the Spirit of unity, gives its all to the cause of peace on earth, good will among men.

*Not until we become true brothers and sisters.* No peace until we believe the song that the little children sing:

> Red and yellow, black and white
> They are precious in His sight
> Jesus loves the little children of the world.

No peace until we understand that human brotherhood is a very broad category, including our family in Christ and our larger family in Adam.

Do you remember that wonderful rabbi who was asked by his student, "Why in the beginning did God just make Adam and Eve?" He answered, "That's so that nobody could ever say to anybody else: 'I come from better stock than you do.' "

I used to believe we would treat each other better if we could just realize God made us all, hence we are one huge human family. I confess I don't believe it any more. Too many wars, too much inhumanity in my brief lifetime alone convinced me otherwise. Perhaps we're all like the Bedouins of whom Chaim Potok has written, describing their devotion to the "razzia," the lightening raid upon a neighboring tribe or village. Its purpose was to steal as much as possible with as little bloodshed as possible. Although if blood must be shed, so be it. Potok quotes a poet who lived during the early period of Islamic conquest:

> Our business is to make raids on the enemy, on our neighbor and on our brother, in case we find none to raid but a brother.[9]

So much for brotherhood!

Our own nation doesn't escape the shame. In Front Royal, Virginia, a sign was erected:

> On May 23, 1862, the Maryland First Regiment CSA [Confederate States of America] opposed in this village the Maryland First Regiment USA. Believed to be the only time in the Civil War in which the divided halves of a single regiment fought each other.[10]

In that battle, brother fought brother, townsman fought

townsman; boys who grew up with each other pointed their gun barrels at one another.

How often I've thanked God for opportunities to go abroad. He has shown me through travel what I hadn't yet learned through books or classrooms. In other countries, I may be with people of black or yellow or red skin, but they are indeed my brothers and sisters. They see with eyes like mine. They taste with tongues like mine. They hear with ears like mine. They feel with fingers like mine. Their hearts beat like mine. And God loves them as He loves me. When I learn of war or rumors of war in the nations I have visited, I grieve, for I have family there. You can't be indifferent when people are shooting at your family!

Of the Christian family within the human family, Paul writes, "Let the peace of Christ rule in your hearts, since as members of one body you were called to peace" (Col. 3:15), and "Make every effort to keep the unity of the Spirit through the bond of peace" (Eph. 4:3). Brotherhood has to start somewhere. Let it start among brothers and sisters in Christ — and permeate outwardly into every village and nation.

*Not until reason replaces passion.* Ancient Semites worshiped Astarte, goddess of love and war. We agree, don't we? "All's fair in love and war," we contend. By that truism we mean there are certain areas of our lives where passion, not reason, rules. And when passion is in charge, anything goes! Peace and passion seldom co-exist.

In 1910 Norman Angell published his provocative book, *The Great Illusion*, to prove modern warfare had become so dangerous no one could emerge a winner; the victor would be as damaged as the vanquished. Since nobody could win, he argued, nobody would go to war. War had become obsolete. That was 1910. It was a very popular book, translated into eleven languages. Study groups on the book were formed in various places because of its wonderful, rational argument against war.

Since 1910 the United States alone has shed soldiers' blood in World War I, World War II, Korea, Vietnam, Granada, Nicaragua, Panama, Lebanon, and who really knows where else? As we noted elsewhere, mankind has fought more wars in this century than in any other comparable period of time in history. Why? Not because we don't know it's wrong, wasteful and stupid. Sometimes there were reasons. Other times, we just became angry or greedy. Passion took charge. The rule of the playground was applied. The child takes over, reason withdraws and the clinched fist and sharp tongue attack.

My wife Joy and I still laugh at one of her retorts during a rather heated family discussion (you might have thought it was an argument). When we were younger (much, much younger), Joy and I were capable of some pretty lively discussions, always over nothing of real importance. (I can't remember a single heated disagreement we have had in thirty years over anything worth getting heated up over.) We just felt like fighting, I guess. We were in the midst of this particular conflict when I said to her in my quiet, temperate way, "Woman, be reasonable."

"You know I can't be reasonable when I'm mad," she answered. She can't, either. Neither can I.

Neither can the rest of humanity.

That's why there will not be peace until reason replaces passion.

*In other words, not so long as we take the easy way.* Unfortunately, war is much simpler than peace, at home or abroad. North Korean's Pham Van Dong says his country learned this lesson well.

> "Yes, we defeated the United States but now we are plagued by problems. We do not have enough to eat. We are a poor, underdeveloped nation. Waging war is simple but running a country is very difficult."[11]

There's only one word, then, that remains to be said on the subject.

*There will not be peace until we try it Jesus' way.* I have been helped to think through this subject by a former Polish ambassador to the United States, whose autobiography held me in thrall for all its 672 pages. I have been earnestly following Poland's affairs since visiting there during their 1982 famine. Romuald Spasowski helped me understand what I had seen then; more pointedly, I was inspired by his odyssey toward the Christian faith. He was brought up to be a model Communist by his father, a Marxist professor committed to communism as the only hope for workers and for world peace. Imperialists, capitalists, had to be defeated.

For quite idealistic reasons, then, young Romuald became a Communist and entered government service, rising to serve as ambassador in several different countries, including two terms in America. For forty years he labored in the foreign service, but he became increasingly cynical as Russia exploited his native Poland. He felt empty. His son committed suicide; his family was nearly destroyed by his own infidelity. He knew he was being spied on, his phones tapped, his every move under surveillance. What galled him was that Christians, including his wife, demonstrated a strength he didn't have.

Finally, he defected. All those years of serving the cause of world peace had come to naught. His life had been lived in vain. Only the Polish church, he had to confess, had truly fought for the Polish people.

The last paragraph of his book gripped me. "The greatest day of my life came on April 9, 1985." He publicly accepted Christ as Lord. "I asked myself whether I deserved the grace of forgiveness and reconciliation with Him who liberated man's greatest hope. In joining myself to Christ, I felt at last at one with Poland's martyred people."[11]

He couldn't make peace through Communism, or governmental negotiations or any other form of human power struggle. He found personal peace when he, a lifelong Communist, gave himself to Christ. He joined the church of his countrymen, because in the Roman Catholic Church he had observed people who had attained personal peace working for the peace of all people in Jesus' name.

I have brought this chapter to a conclusion with the story of one man, because in the beginning, peace is personal. Jesus made peacemaking an individual matter, something to be undertaken by each peacemaker. The evidence from scripture and everyday life is the same: In this world we have trouble, but Christ gives peace and charges us to be peacemakers.

So we shall be.

Isaiah 2:3-5
Matthew 5:9; 10:34-39; 24:6-8
Luke 4:16-20
John 14:27; 16:33
I Corinthians 13:11
Ephesians 2:14-22

**Endnotes**

1. Quoted in Alaistair Cooke, *The Americans*. England and New York: Penguin Books, co. 1979, p. 58.

**2.** *The Mesa Tribune*, January 12, 1988, p. A13.

**3.** Dan Kurzman, *Day of the Bomb*. London: Weidenfeld and Nicolson, Publishers, co. 1986, p. 416.

**4.** Norman Cousins, *Human Options*. New York, London: W.W. Norton and Company, co. 1981, p. 138.

**5.** Dan Kurzman, *Day of the Bomb*. London: Weidenfeld and Nicolson, Publishers, co. 1986, pp. 355-356.

**6.** Page Smith, *America Enters the World*. New York, et al: McGraw-Hill Book Co., co. 1985, p. 460.

**7.** Stanley Karnow, *Vietnam*. New York: The Viking Press, co. 1983, p. 396.

**8.** Robert Eels and Bartell Nyberg, *Lonely Walk*. Portland, Oregon: Multnomah Press, co. 1979, p. 133.

**9.** *Wandering, Chaim Potok's History of the Jews*. New York: Fawcett Crest, Pub., co. 1978, p. 330.

**10.** Norman B. Rohrer, *The Poor Man Cried: The Story of Larry Ward*. Tyndale House, co. 1984, p. 87.

**11.** Stanley Karnow, *Vietnam*. New York: The Viking Press, co. 1983, p. 9.

**12.** Romuald Spasowski, *The Liberation of One*. San Diego, et al: Harcourt Brace & Jovanovich, Publishers (A Harvest / HBJ Book), co. 1986, p. 672.

# 5

# Will Man Ever Love His Fellow Man?

Will man ever love his fellow man? Based on the evidence presented by history to date, it doesn't seem very likely, does it? If forced to answer the question as stated, we'll have to say, "No, we haven't any hope that human beings, without divine intervention, will learn to love one another." We're too insecure, too greedy, too competitive for love.

We don't want to leave this question too soon, though. Buried in it is another, far more pertinent one: "Will *I, this one person out of the whole race,* ever learn to love *my* fellow man?" If I can, then there's reason for some optimism about the race.

This very personal question implies many others: Will I ever become as concerned for another's welfare as I am for my own? Will I be willing to sacrifice my profit for the wellbeing of others? Can I ever rid myself of blinding prejudices? Will I become able to love enough to give to someone in need without first feeling compelled to pass judgment on him? Am I forgiving? Loving one's fellow man — even just one person — is no small order, is it?

Jesus' famous parable of the Good Samaritan identifies the person I must love. He's my neighbor. ("Love your neighbor as yourself.")

The Lord tells the story for the sake of a calculating lawyer. "Who is my neighbor?" the man asks Jesus, undoubtedly looking for a loophole (Luke 10:25-37). He wants "to justify himself." (Who doesn't?) His prior question, "What must I do to inherit eternal life?" betrays his selfish concern. He's not really worried about his or anybody's neighbor. As far as he's concerned, salvation is a private matter. So it is for most of us, I suspect.

Jesus takes a dim view of our self-centeredness. He refuses to allow His disciples to ignore their fellow human beings. In effect, he redefines "neighbor" to include anybody, anywhere, who needs us. If we would follow Him, not only must we "love the Lord our God with all our heart and soul and mind and strength," a command we readily accept, but we must also offer the same respect to our neighbor, a less popular consideration.

## Start Where You Are

Jesus' simple but pointed story defines "neighbor" in the most inclusive manner possible. He (or she) is any person who is at the moment near us, in our "neighborhood." We carry our neighborhood around with us. Thus our neighbor can be found anywhere we go, on a road to any Jericho, in any kind of peril. There's no escape: we must "neighbor" where we are, with whoever needs us.

The priest and the Levite, not one whit less interested in religion than the probing lawyer, are so immersed in their duties (or egos or schedules) they can't be bothered with the victim. They have appointments to keep, people to see, places to go, things to do. They are religious, all right, but religion by itself does not give us eyes to see what God sees.

If we are going to be neighborly in Jesus' terms, we must

1. Look at and *see* our neighbor's plight.

2. Identify with him in his need. No strutting superiority, please. No smuggly uttered, "There but for the grace of God go I." It wasn't lack of God's grace that spurred the robbers' attack.

3. Refuse to dismiss the person with a label. Labels blind the vision and soothe the conscience. "Careless fool, he had no business out here." "Hmph, another bum." "Not my kind." "Just another drunk."

4. Stop. Don't pass by. It becomes a habit after while, passing by another's helplessness. Courtesy, if nothing more, dictates at least the honest query, the proferred hand. When there are so many beggars and bums, one becomes hardened and walks on. Understandable, but unneighborly.

5. Be pro-life, not in a political sense but in a Christian one. Know that the God who created and sustains life wants it saved. The sanctity of persons must be protected wherever.

## Examine Your Religion

What does your religion insist is your top responsibility? As He tells the story, Jesus holds up the priest and the Levite as symbols of the highest, most respectable kind of religiosity. They are good men, people like our fulltime church workers busy, about the work of the Lord, pressed on every side by important duties. They aren't especially calloused, just preoccupied with valued responsibilities. They would stop if they could to help this half-naked, half-dead victim. But they can't. Oh, of their religious respectability there is no doubt; they just don't love him.

Among the several dangers of religion is its capacity for doing us as much harm as good. I'm shaken every time I read the statistics, and I read them again just recently, that in recent years an average of 330,000 Christians are being martyred around the world annually. Because of their religion — and usually because of their enemy's religion — they die. Religion kills. This is why Jesus gave His disciples a *new commandment*, "Love one another. As I have loved you, so you must love one another." He didn't limit His injunction to just mutual affection, either: "Love your enemies and pray for those who persecute you, that you may be sons of your Father in heaven" (John 13:34; Matt. 5:44-45). For Jesus' disciples, the religious question cannot ever merely echo the lawyer's, "What must I do to inherit eternal life — for me, irrespective of anybody else?" There can be no "irrespective." So examine your religion. Is love its core?

## Examine Your Prejudices

Jesus' audience must have been stunned when they realized He was making a hated Samaritan the hero of His parable. Jesus' choice is deliberate. He's talking to Jews, who as a rule hated Samaritans. The racial prejudice separating these geographical neighbors (and spiritual cousins) could only be compared with similar feelings between whites and blacks in the worst era of America's indefensible race relations. The despicable Samaritan, not the righteous Jewish religious leaders, is Jesus' model neighbor.

To this day Jesus' little story makes us squirm, doesn't it? He still asks of his audience, "What are your prejudices? Can you love those of another color? Can you love those of another culture? Can you love those who don't think, act, walk, talk, sound, smell, sing, look like you?"

We are usually not very discerning about our own biases, but they are there. Every society fosters its own brand of prejudice. We "pre-judge" every person we meet, as an "insider" or an "outsider." My friends in Prince Edward Island had fun explaining that in their province, everyone is either from there or "from away." Period. It's a convenient, shorthand way to think. But it can be deadly. If I belong to some "in" group, I am protected. If I am merely human, I am at risk.

I am an American, so I have a nation to defend me.

I am a Christian, so I have a church to defend me.

I am a Republican or Democrat, so my party defends me.

I am a human being. Who defends me?

We cluster in human groups to find safety with our own kind. But what about people who have nobody to protect them? When a man on a journey is beaten and robbed, who rises to his defense? Who can always stay in where it's safe? When a person is slandered, is hurt, who protests on his behalf? Don't you find it instructive that nations have national anthems but there are no anthems for humanity? Who cares about humanity?

My own narrow thinking became evident during my college teaching days. For a few years I directed Milligan College's Humanities program, as fascinating and fulfilling an assignment as I have ever had. Our goal was to understand the development of Western Civilization as expressed in its art, music, philosophy, language, literature, and history. A challenging breadth of disciplines, to be sure, and I rejoiced as my knowledge of our heritage broadened. Then one day I woke up to a disturbing fact. We were totally ignoring Asian, African, South American and several other civilizations, acting as if over half of the world didn't exist. Our perspective was blinded by our national experience; what impinged on the history of the United States of America mattered. What didn't, didn't. Unwittingly, we had built a bias into our humanities program.

Ours is an often noble inheritance, to be certain. I'm proud to be an American. But God loves the whole world and designed it to be one global neighborhood. He looks upon all mankind without prejudice; He causes "his sun to rise on the evil and the good, and sends rain on the righteous and the unrighteous" (Matt. 5:45). His love for His creatures is not limited to one or another civilization. Nor can ours be.

While musing on my cultural myopia, it has been humbling for me to read a speech that the famous Sioux Indian Chief Sitting Bull addressed to his people back in 1877. His neighborhood was as large as mine was small.

> See, Brothers, spring is here.
> The earth has taken the embrace of the sun,
> And soon we will see the children of that love.

All seeds are awake, and all animals.
From this great power we, too, have our lives.
And therefore we concede to our fellow creatures,
Even our animal fellows, the same right as
Ourselves to live on this earth.[1]

In Sitting Bull's remarkably embracing, unprejudiced statement we hear echoes of the Psalmist's equally reverent hymn:

> The earth is the Lord's, and everything in it, the world, and all who live in it (Psa. 24:1).

So we who want life as Christ would have us, must remove the blinders of prejudice so that looking, we can see.

Just how far will your love go? Can you love the guys in the head office? The dirty fellow on the street asking for a handout? The busy, snobbish businesswoman? The weird looking teenagers with their straight hair and curled lips? How far will your love go? What barriers of prejudice must be broken?

## Examine Your Priorities

The Samaritan was a businessman. He had appointments to keep, money to make, important affairs to attend to. Taking care of a wounded man was inconvenient and costly, yet he momentarily set aside his personal business for the more urgent demands of the victim. His charity challenges our sense of priorities, doesn't it? The rescuer is acting out Paul's injunction:

> Make my joy complete by being likeminded, having the same love, being one in spirit and purpose. Do nothing out

> of selfish ambition or vain conceit, but in humility consider others better than yourselves. Each of you should look not only to your own interests, but also to the interests of others (Phil. 2:2-4).

Some years ago Dennis W. Jones tried other ways to express his love for the Lord, with uncertain results.

> Oh, God,
> The sign said smile if you love Jesus;
> so I smiled all day long,
> and people thought I was a staff worker for
> Jimmy Carter.
> The sign said honk if you love Jesus;
> so I honked,
> and a policeman arrested me for disturbing the
> peace in a hospital quiet zone.
> The sign said wave if you love Jesus;
> so I waved both hands;
> but I lost control of the car,
> and crashed into the back of a Baptist bus.
>
> O God,
> if I cannot smile,
> or honk,
> or wave,
> how will Jesus know I love Him?[2]

He might try what Jesus recommended to Peter.

The occasion was the very end of Jesus' ministry, along the banks of the Sea of Galilee. After fishing all night, Peter and six other disciples had nothing to show for their efforts. Jesus called to them from shore, directing them to try the other side of their boat. Their catch was greater than their nets could hold.

Back on shore Jesus fed them breakfast. He had something more than food in mind, however. He wanted to reinstate Peter, who had abandoned Him at His trial.

Three times Peter denied Jesus; three times Jesus questioned Peter.

> "Simon son of John, do you truly love me more than these?"
> Yes, Lord, you know that I love you."
> "Feed my lambs."
> Again Jesus said, "Simon son of John, do you truly love me?"
> Jesus said, "Take care of my sheep."
> He answered, "Yes, Lord, you know that I love you."
> The third time he said to him, "Simon son of John, do you love me?"
> Peter was hurt because Jesus asked him the third time, "Do you love me?" He said, "Lord, you know all things; you know that I love you."
> Jesus said, "Feed my sheep" (John 21:15-17).

Before tending to your business affairs, even when it's inconvenient, certainly when it's needed, no matter where you are, no matter when, "Feed my sheep." That sheep is your neighbor.

## Love With God's Love

During the first World War a German soldier, bayonet fixed, jumped into a shell hole behind the front lines. To his horror he discovered an English soldier, severely wounded. He'd been trained to attack. He was supposed to kill the enemy, but something in the Englishman's pitiful condition stopped him.

In the impasse the English soldier asked for a drink and the German, his humanitarian instincts aroused, gave him one from his canteen. The wounded man's look expressed his thanks, and then, more by gestures than by words, he asked the German to get his wallet out of his uniform. The soldier complied, dropping several pictures as he did. With conspicious tenderness the dying man looked at his wife and children.

Those few moments transformed the German soldier's attitude. The man he saw before him now was no longer the enemy but a fellow human being, a husband who would be mourned, a father who would be sorely missed. A human being, one of Jesus' sheep.

A season or two ago I went skiing. For weeks afterward I wore evidence of the excursion on my hand. When people asked me what happened (and they invariably did), I told them. " There's a sign by the ski lift, just as you get on the chair, that says, 'Thou shalt not descend the slopes on thy thumb.' But I didn't see that sign until I had already violated the warning." Amazing how far you can go on a thumb, actually, if you balance right.

My mistake was in skiing with youngsters. My buddies were our church's business administrator Mike, 31, our "adopted" son Brian, 25, and our son Lane, 20. Back home I told my wife, "I need older playmates." Young ones are too hard on the body.

Anyway, we went skiing. That is, they went skiing and I tried. It was only my second attempt ever. In two days, Mike didn't fall once. Brian only fell once. Lane took a few more tumbles. I fell once in honor of every skier there.

While lunching at the lodge we talked briefly with Gordy Gray, the youth minister at a sister church on the northwest side of Phoenix. We learned he had brought some members of the Pacific Christian College Chorale for an outing. Since my daughter was a part of the chorale I hoped she was skiing. It turned out she wasn't, to my disappointment.

When we finished eating, we returned to the slopes for our afternoon skiing, looking unsuccessfully for the chorale group. As we were standing in line to take the ski lift up to the top, the Ski Patrol brought an accident victim by on a toboggan. I couldn't see her face, but it was obvious from the care she was receiving the young woman had taken a bad spill. I felt sorry for her. I knew how easy it is to get into that position, having barely escaped disaster several times that morning myself.

The next day, once more ascending the ski lift, I was doubled on the chair with a young lady who works on the slopes. I asked her about the accident. She told me what had happened. The girl, an inexperienced skier, had ridden the lift up to the top of a run (one I had been trying to conquer). It's a mean slope for a beginner. She planted her feet at the top of the slope, headed her skis straight ahead and took off.

She immediately realized she made a terrible mistake. People heard her screaming as she whizzed by them, "Help me, help me." Of course nobody could, until she stopped. The simplest thing to do in a situation like that is to throw yourself off, to cause yourself to fall. But she couldn't make herself do it. Down the mountainside she flew, faster and faster, crying for help, until at the bottom she crashed into a telephone pole and snapped her leg.

I felt terrible. I had seen her and almost felt as if I knew her.

In a moment I was wending my own way down the mountainside.

Back in Phoenix the next morning our daughter Candy called. I told her about looking for her up at the ski resort. She said, "One of our girls broke her leg."

"What?"

"Didn't you hear about Tiffany?"

"Tiffany who?"

"Tiffany Larsen."

I couldn't believe it. The girl on the toboggan was the daughter of my friend, Jim Larsen, a fellow minister in Tucson. I was devastated. I knew her. I know her family. We've been together. Suddenly I cared.

Over this one incident I had experienced three levels of feeling:

First, "Oh, isn't that a shame? Somebody got hurt."

Then, "Isn't that terrible? I could have been the one. I've been trying to master that slope all morning."

Finally, with genuine empathy, "Oh, no, I know her. Her dad and I are friends!"

The first level was casual. Something interesting had happened to somebody. Pity.

At the second level I identified with her. I could picture myself on that toboggan, having fallen once too often in my unique, clumsy style. I hurt for her. I was glad "somebody" did something about her need. Sympathy.

The third level moved beyond caring to action. Had I known then what I discovered later, I'd have been beside Tiffany, offering to do anything I could, acting out my concern.

My levels of relating to Tiffany in her distress were, I'm afraid, pretty common. We have learned to distance ourselves from the hurts of the people we don't know. When our consciences prick us, we justify our aloofness, but with a little defensiveness: "I can't help everybody, for heaven's sake."

When the victims have names and we know their faces and have some relationship with them, though, our whole attitude changes. We want to come to their rescue. The difference within us is in our seeing our relationship with them.

What would Jesus have us do? He wants us to look at others closely, individually, discerning each to be a person of value to the Lord, hence to us. As a Good Shepherd loves His sheep, so the Lord loves this one. If we love Him, we love His sheep.

"What must I do to have eternal life?" the lawyer asked Jesus. The man already knew the answer: "Love the Lord your God with all your heart and with all your soul and with all your strength and with all your mind." "Love your neighbor as yourself." He also knew the crux of the issue was in accurately determining exactly who was his neighbor.

What he didn't know was the size of his neighborhood.

Luke 10:25-37
John 21:15-17
I Corinthians 13
I John 3:11-18; 4:7-21

**Endnotes**

1. Alex Shoumatoff, *The Mountain of Names*. New York: Simon and Schuster, co. 1985, p. 54
2. *The Christian Century*, October 27, 1976.

# 6
# When Will The World End?

I don't know when the world will end. Neither does anybody else. Jesus Himself says we can't know (Matt. 24:36). Even His authoritative voice doesn't stop our speculation, though, if we can judge by the popularity of prophecy sermons and books like Hal Lindsey's *The Late Great Planet Earth,* which has sold well over fifteen million copies since it was published in the 1970's. *New York Times* named Lindsay the best-selling author of the decade, a tribute less to Lindsay's scholarship than to the public's appetite.

Fascination with the end didn't originate in the 1970's, however. Ever since Jesus' ascension His disciples have eagerly awaited His return, with end-times fervor reaching fever pitch in three periods: the first century, when the young church confidently expected His imminent appearance; the end of the tenth century, with the anticipation of a new millennium with the year A.D. 1000; and the nineteenth-twentieth centuries.

This latest era has been variously explained. The aftermath of the French Revolution ignited a new interest in prophecy in Europe in the 1800's. Bible students, observing the decline of papal power and the growth of the secular state (with its accompanying rise of interest in religion) reread the books of Daniel and Revelation to discern the signs of the times. In the United States, groups majoring in end-times prophecy arose, such as the Jehovah's Witnesses, the Millerites (Seventh Day Adventists), and the Mormons ("Latter Day Saints"). Even a group with a far different agenda, dedicated to a new reformation of the church, echoed the popular interest in the world's conclusion. Alexander Campbell, leader of this Restoration Movement, named his publication the *Millennial Harbinger.*

The pioneering Seventh Day Adventists' leader, William Miller, set 1843 for the return of Jesus Christ. The Lord's refusal to appear did not put an end to the Millerites, whose numbers are larger than ever at the end of the twentieth century.

Preacher Charles Taize Russell founded the Jehovah's Witnesses. He preached that the six thousand years of man's existence on earth had ended in 1872 and that the glorified Christ became invisibly present in 1874. During the next forty years God's saints would be "harvested," until on October 1, 1914, it would be all over for Gentiles (non-Witnesses). On that date the evil worldly system would collapse and God would have His everlasting day. He was wrong, but his movement persists.

During this same century an Englishman named John Nelson Darby put the finishing touches on his premillennial theory, which was later popularized in the Scofield

Reference Bible. Darby believed the Second Coming will be preceded by an obvious social, economic, political and family deterioration. Since those conditions can be discerned in practically every era, it is no wonder that Bible believing Christians have pointed with alarm or eagerness to degenerating morals in every human sphere and proclaimed, "This is it!"

An important twentieth-century symbol has been the establishing of a new political state, Israel, which many premillennialists equate with the restoration of ancient Israel. They believe the people of Israel will be in Palestine at the time of Christ's return. They hailed the 1917 Balfour Declaration permitting Jews to settle in Palestine as the fulfillment of Jeremiah 29:14:

> "I will be found by you," declares the Lord, "and will bring you back from captivity. I will gather you from all the nations and places where I have banished you," declares the Lord, "and will bring you back to the place from which I carried you into exile."

The formal establishment of the nation of Israel on May 14, 1948, further convinced premillennialists. Hal Lindsey dates the start of the countdown to the end from this moment. When the Israelis occupied Jerusalem in 1967, the victory was hailed as further proof that these are, indeed, the very last days.

Premillennialists give the most confident answer to the question, "When will the world end?" Every piece of bad news, either domestic or foreign, is additional evidence helping to prove their contention that the world is about finished. They are quick to point out the perceived rise in incidences of earthquakes, famines, floods, volcanoes and increasing turbulence in the world political scene. If nations are at war with one another, they point to war as proof; if they seem to be getting along (or even reuniting, like East and West Germany), they speak fearfully of a one-world government. The rise (or fall) of the dollar, increases in abortions, proliferation of pornography in print and on film, homosexual militancy, breakdown of families, nuclear arms in the hands of a growing number of nations, and other items in a long list of human ills are proof positive that we are well along the homestretch toward the end.

Since the Antichrist is expected at the end, every outburst of end-times fever has produced its own villian. In the first century, Nero was nominated. In the nineteenth century, Napoleon was often given the honor. The twentieth century has produced a bumper crop, including Mussolini, Hitler, Stalin, Kissinger, and even Anwar Sadat. Since the label has been pinned on so many, the wary Christian is wise to avoid playing this naming game.

## What We Know for Sure

In light of the fact so many prophets have been so wrong in the past, what can we believe for certain about the end of the world? Which prophet should we believe?

How about Jesus?

*"No one knows about that day or hour."* We can't know much of anything, if we are to believe Jesus. "Not even the angels in heaven, nor the Son, but only the Father" knows "about that hour" (Read Matthew 24, especially v. 36). Jesus isn't the only one to caution us. Here is II Peter 3:10:

> But the day of the Lord will come like a thief. The heavens

> will disappear with a roar; the elements will be destroyed by fire, and the earth and everything in it will be laid bare.

Another familiar passage is I Thessalonians 5:1-3, which the Apostle Paul wrote very early in the development of the first century church:

> Now, brothers, about times and dates we do not need to write to you, for you know very well that the day of the Lord will come like a thief in the night. While people are saying, "Peace and safety," destruction will come on them suddenly, as labor pains on a pregnant woman, and they will not escape.

Jesus uses the same figure of speech, "like a thief." He also speaks of a household servant whose master "will come on a day when he does not expect him and at an hour he is not aware of" (Matt. 24:50).

The Bible could not be more explicit. We don't know.

Scripture doesn't stop some people, however. In Grannis, Arkansas, on June 30, 1976, an eager two dozen of Elizabeth Nance Bard's disciples stood waiting for earth's demise. She had prophecied Jesus' return on that day. Her reasoning was simple. She expected Him on that day because it was the nine-month anniversary of the beginning of the vigil to await the Second Coming of Christ. "From conception to birth is nine months," she noted. (If this doesn't quite make sense to you, don't despair. I can't follow her reasoning either.)

Even when He didn't come, the group didn't lose faith. "Everything is in the hands of God. We know He will provide. We are not worried. We are just as sure as ever that He will come. We just know it." A little less certainly, Elizabeth Nance Bard added that the world might not end for everyone at the same time.[1]

Christians are not the only persons susceptible to millennial mania. At the beginning of the 1990's, a 33,000-acre region in Montana's Paradise Valley was invaded by members of the Church Universal and Triumphant, New Agers whose belief is a mixture of Christian and Eastern religions. Led by Elizabeth Clare Prophet, at least two thousand disciples prepared 46 steel-and-concrete bunkers hollowed out of the mountainous depths with stores of dry food, flashlights, medical supplies, and other essentials. They came from the United States, South America, and Europe because their prophet convinced them the end is imminent.[2]

There's nothing new in this hysteria. As I have said, sages in almost every age have bewailed the world's deteriorating conditions and hailed the imminent end of everything. These words, spoken in Carthage in A.D. 250, have their echoes in every other era I have studied:

> Who cannot see that the world is already in its decline and no longer has the strength and vigor of former times? There is less rain in winter to encourage the growth of seeds; springtime is not now so enjoyable nor autumn so fruitful; the quarries, as if from weariness, give less stone and marble and the gold and silver mines are already worked out; the land remains untilled, the seas lack pilots and the armies are without men; there is less innocence in the courts, less justice in the judges, less concord between friends, less artistic sincerity, less moral strictness.[3]

*"Therefore keep watch."* Since so many have been so concerned and so wrong for so long, should we simply ignore the subject? Not at all. Hear Jesus out. Even though He warns us we cannot know when, at the same time He also advises us to be on the alert. It's going to be as it was "in the days of Noah."

> For in the days before the flood, people were eating and drinking, marrying and giving in marriage, up to the day Noah entered the ark; and they knew nothing about what would happen until the flood came and took them all away. That is how it will be at the coming of the Son of Man. Two men will be in the field; one will be taken and the other left. Two women will be grinding with a hand mill; one will be taken and the other left (Matt. 24:38-41. See also Genesis 6 and 7).

I chuckle every time I see one of those bumper stickers: "Warning! In Case of Rapture, This Car Will Have No Driver." It'll be just that sudden, Jesus says. Without warning.

> Therefore keep watch, because you do not know on what day your Lord will come. But understand this: If the owner of the house had known at what time of night the thief was coming, he would have kept watch and would not have let his house be broken into. So you also must be ready, because the Son of Man will come at an hour when you do not expect him. (Matt. 24:42-44).

What does He mean, "Be ready?" Are we to sell all we have, camp on a mountaintop and wait for Him to swoop down and pick us up? No, that is quite clearly the opposite of what He means. He is urging us to so live that if we should die today, we are prepared to enter into eternity with Him. So live that if you should die and go to heaven, there's a reason to admit you. So live that if He should come unexpectedly this day, there is no barrier between you, no breach in your relationship with Him. You have accepted His grace, you have turned your life over to Him, you are living for Him now as you want to live for Him forever. So live that when He comes He'll find you doing His will.

Read a few verses ahead, into Matthew 25. There you will find Jesus' famous parable of the foolish and wise bridesmaids. It is among the best commentaries for Matthew 24 to be found anywhere. Note there the enjoyment of the five prepared bridesmaids; note also the unfortunate consequences that befell the careless ones. Jesus provides his own moral, in language identical to Matthew 24:42: "Therefore, keep watch."

*We must be faithful.* Wise is the servant whose returning master finds him on the job, honestly fulfilling his assignment.

> Who then is the faithful and wise servant, whom the master has put in charge of the servants in his household to give them their food at the proper time? It will be good for that servant whose master finds him doing so when he returns (Matt. 24:45-46).

God has given all of us authority to manage the gifts and resources He has entrusted to us: money, possessions, abilities, occupation, influence, time. What He requires is our faithfulness. He certainly doesn't want us abandoning our responsibilities, high-tailing it to some mountain retreat or lookout point, waiting in eagerness for His appearing. If the Lord should return tomorrow, He wants to find us at our jobs, doing our duties, wisely administering of our affairs, living for Him daily. Then we cannot be surprised and we'll have no reason to be afraid. We'll be at our posts when He comes.

Here's Paul's advice:

> But mark this: There will be terrible times in the last days. People will be lovers of themselves, lovers of money, boastful, proud, abusive, disobedient to their parents, ungrateful, unholy, without love, unforgiving, slanderous,

> without self-control, brutal, not lovers of the good, treacherous, rash, conceited, lovers of pleasure rather than lovers of God — having a form of godliness but denying its power. Have nothing to do with them (II Tim. 3:1-5).

Be faithful, even if you are the only one who is. Do not fall into the ways of this world — especially if you believe, as some people lament, "things are getting worse and worse."

Peter calls for living a special kind of life:

> But the day of the Lord will come like a thief. The heavens will disappear with a roar; the elements will be destroyed by fire, and the earth and everything in it will be laid bare. Since everything will be destroyed in this way, what kind of people ought you to be? You ought to live holy and godly lives as you look forward to the day of God and speed its coming (II Pet. 3:10-12a).

The Apostle Paul also urges Christians to enlightened living:

> It is God's will that you should be holy; that you should avoid sexual immorality; that each of you should learn to control his own body in a way that is holy and honorable, not in passionate lust like the heathen who do not know God. . . . But you, brothers, are not in darkness so that this day should surprise you like a thief. You are all sons of the light and sons of the day. We do not belong to the night or to the darkness. So then, let us not be like others, who are asleep, but let us be alert and self-controlled. For those who sleep, sleep at night, and those who get drunk, get drunk at night. But since we belong to the day, let us be self-controlled, putting on faith and love as a breastplate, and the hope of salvation as a helmet (I Thess. 4:3-6a; 5:4-8).

These verses need no explanation, do they? Unfortunately,

this aspect of end-times discussions we like to skip over. We're fascinated with speculation about the signs of the times and we're captivated by anybody who will give us reason to believe these are the last days, but we show much less eagerness to reform ourselves to get ready. Some are even gullible enough to follow the latest of the pied pipers who regularly appear to pipe in yet another well-calculated date as THE day of Jesus' appearing: 1993. Others succumb to the temptation to rejoice over the latest catastrophe; it means, "we're just that much closer now." Such well-intentioned believers seem unaware how clearly out of the will of the Lord such speculating and ill-wishing is. Jesus wants something far different of us. He urges faithfulness, watchfulness, obedience — holiness! Thus it is incumbent upon us to live every day in such a way that, if Christ were to come today, we would be ready to live with Him forever, having been found faithfully at our work.

## Some Things Are Certain

*The Lord will return in glory.* How God will bring earthly existence to a close remains uncertain, in spite of the many scholarly guesses at our disposal. Precisely how the Lord will return is also beyond the comprehension of at least this writer. What is certain, however, is that the Bible promises what we call His Second Coming:

> For the grace of God that brings salvation has appeared to all men. It teaches us to say 'No' to ungodliness and worldly passions, and to live self-controlled, upright and godly lives in this present age, while we wait for the blessed hope — the glorious appearing of our great God and Savior, Jesus Christ . . . (Titus 2:11-13).

Our hope is therefore in the Lord and not in any proposed timetable.

> Just as man is destined to die once, and after that to face judgment, so Christ was sacrificed once to take away the sins of many people; and he will appear a second time, not to bear sin, but to bring salvation to those who are waiting for Him (Heb. 9:27-28).

So we wait. And we watch. And we work.

Matthew 24:36-46; 25:1-13
I Thessalonians 5:1-11
II Timothy 3:1-5
Titus 2:11-13
Hebrews 9:27, 28
II Peter 3:10-13

**Endnotes**

**1.** Associated Press, quoted in William Griffin, *Endtime: The Doomsday Catalog*. New York: Collier Books, co. 1979, p. 57.

**2.** "Heading for the Hills," *TIME*, March 26, 1990, p. 20. *TIME* also notes the Prophet had warned that California would fall into the sea in 1987.

**3.** Cyprian of Carthage in William Griffin, *Endtime: The Doomsday Catalogue.* New York: Collier Books, co. 1979, p. 54.

# 7

# What Does The Future Hold?

Back in 1967, the December 31 issue of the Arizona *Republic* included a special section headlined

Make a Date for the Millennium, January 1, 2000
Most of Us Will Live to See It
What Sort of a World Will It Be?

Beneath the headline the article speculated tantalizingly about the nature of our world in A.D. 2000:

— Longer life, with two careers per lifetime.

— Birth control and artificial insemination would lead to the destruction of traditional marriage and family ties.

— Absolute control of man's personality and behavior by electronic devices and drugs.

— Automated or more mechanized housekeeping and house maintenance.

— Relatively effective appetite and weight control.

— Improved chemical control of some mental illnesses and some aspects of senility.

All of these and more possibilities await us in just a few short years.

I enjoyed reading the article, but I didn't take its prognostications too seriously. Sometimes prophets are just plain wrong. When their bold pronouncements are read years after the fact, they can provide some pretty delightful enjoyment.

For example, away back in the year 1839, Dr. Alfred Velpeau grumped before the introduction of anesthesia, "It is absurb to go on seeking [the abolishment of pain in surgery]. *Knife* and *pain* are two words in surgery that must forever be associated in the consciousness of the patient. To this compulsory combination we shall have to adjust ourselves." Just seven short years would prove him wrong.

Then there was Lee DeForest, the American inventor who has been called "Father of the Radio." He pontificated in 1926, "While theoretically and technically television may be feasible, commercially and financially I consider it an impossibility, a development of which we need waste little time dreaming." You might think of Mr. DeForest next time you watch the Superbowl.

Here's another one. In 1938 *Fortune* Magazine reported, "At present few scientists foresee any serious or practical use for atomic energy. They regard the atom-splitting experiment as useful steps in the attempt to describe the atom more accurately but not as the key to the unlocking of any new power."[1]

They won't hurt you, such prophecies, so long as you can remember they are usually wrong. Predictions about the weather or the state of the economy or even the political alliances among nations are often wildly far from the mark.

You can be certain, then, that anything I might say about the future is suspect. That's why I won't try to answer the question of what the future holds on my own authority. We'll see what the Bible says.

## It Can Hold the Best Part of Your Life

Grow old along with me!
The best is yet to be.
The last of life for which the first was made:
Our times are in His hands,
Who saith, 'A whole I planned,
Youth shows but half; trust God: see all, nor be afraid!'[2]

Of course, Browning's booming optimism is not the only attitude you can take toward your future. William Butler Yeats' famous lines are perhaps a more common appraisal of old age:

An aged man is but a paltry thing,
A tattered coat upon a stick . . . [3]

Well, you can pay your money and take your choice, as the old saying goes. You can look forward to the best or the worst, with anticipation or dread.

## It Holds Trouble and Triumph

To the worrier and the optimist alike Jesus speaks in the Sermon on the Mount. After counseling that worry is futile but trust in the Lord isn't, the Lord urges His disciples to

> seek first his kingdom and his righteousness and all these things will be given to you as well. Therefore do not worry about tomorrow, for tomorrow will worry about itself. Each day has enough trouble of its own (Matt. 6:33-34).

A more even-handed treatment of the future couldn't be desired, could it? On the one hand, worry is unnecessary, because the Lord will provide for those whose priorities are right. On the other, expecting a trouble-free tomorrow is unrealistic.

Being generally a non-worrier (I give up my sleep only reluctantly), I don't dwell much on problems, either mine or someone else's. One weekend's bombardment prompted me to make a list of all the things that I had to deal with in the course of two days:

The mother-in-law of one our pastors died.

One of our churchmen was suddenly hospitalized with an aortic aneurism.

I conducted the wedding (a happy duty) of Catherine DeVaney and Sam Jerrell, a widow and widower in their retirement years.

I counseled a young woman who was angrily leaving home, to her parents grief.

I received word that one of our couples was being divorced.

I was shocked to learn of a situation of child molestation and had to deal with the family's trauma.

While making a deposit at the bank's drive-in window,

one of our men received a severe electrical shock; he faces the loss of the use of his left arm.

Another of our members learned he had a brain tumor; the prognosis was not good.

We launched our Miracle Sunday activities to raise several hundred thousands of dollars for our building project.

We also launched a new Sunday School re-organization program.

Another happy event: an outstanding young couple decided to become members of our church.

Joy and I had to cope with a rather severe crisis regarding one of our own children.

Twelve items in two days and only three of them weren't some kind of "trouble." If that is what I've already been faced with, what will the future hold? Better, worse, or more of the same? I suspect more of the same, don't you?

To regain my balance I occasionally return to Ecclesiastes, chapter 3. It's a good reminder that in this world there is time for everything, and if we live long enough we'll experience it all, the troubles, the triumphs.

> There is a time for everything,
> and a season for every activity under heaven:
> a time to be born and a time to die,
> a time to plant and a time to uproot,
> a time to kill and a time to heal,
> a time to tear down and a time to build,
> a time to weep and a time to laugh,
> a time to mourn and a time to dance,
> a time to scatter stones and a time to gather them,
> a time to embrace and a time to refrain,
> a time to search and a time to give up,

> a time to keep and a time to throw away,
> a time to tear and a time to mend,
> a time to be silent and a time to speak,
> a time to love and a time to hate,
> a time for war and a time for peace.

What then can we say about the future?

## It Holds Change

While reading my favorite section of the newspaper one day, I found just the right answer to our question in the comic strip "Shoe." Cosmo asks his parson whether he has heard any good prayers lately. The padre says he has, as a matter of fact, found a useful prayer. Then he quotes the prayer most of us are well acquainted with.

> God grant me the serenity to accept the things I cannot change, the courage to change the things I *can* change, and the wisdom to know the difference.

Cosmo recalls that he has heard it before. Then the man of the cloth says, "Of course, I like to use the short version: "Lighten up."[4]

We might as well, since change is inevitable, and you can't control it. You can, however, decide how to handle the changes. Bostonians were unnerved in 1857 to read the headline in their Boston *Globe*. "Energy Crisis Looms," it declared, with an even gloomier sub-heading: "World to Go Dark. Whale Blubber Scarce!" Half of the headline was correct; there was a shortage of whale blubber. But it didn't mean darkness for the world. How many similar predictions of imminent disaster have you lived through by now? So have I.

On the other hand, how many unexpected opportunities have you enjoyed? So have I. The same future that holds dread portents also cradles exciting possibilities. The future holds for you an opportunity to grow, to serve, to be significant.

The future holds change for the church as well. A congregation unwilling to change with the times has a very limited future. Some of our church members and I were laughing before a recent morning worship service about the many changes which have shaped our church lately. We never know from Sunday to Sunday what's going to happen next. Our people seem to thrive on the variety. Serious complaints are fairly rare.

Not long before I had been in another state, visiting a church I have known most of my life. What impressed me strongly was how little it has changed over the years. The same people are sitting in their same pews. The order of the service is what I remember from decades before. I could tell you with my eyes closed almost what song we would sing next and then what would happen after that. I knew when to stand and when to sit.

Changes tend to be conservative because human beings are. We like the familiar; we fear the unknown. That's why, even though we know change is inevitable, the future remains scary for us. If we want to enjoy any kind of happiness tomorrow, this one thing we must do: "Lighten up." Change and accept change.

## For Most of Us, the Future Holds Old Age

That is, if we survive all the changes! Thanks to an ever-lengthening life span, the majority of us can now look forward to a long twilight. That could mean a lot of old age. Even people who don't like the thought of growing old would rather grow old than not, even though age forces us to deal with a crumbling physique. We have to accept it. However, evidence is accumulating that we may be able to live physically and mentally vigorous lives far longer than we used to think possible.

Here's one bit of proof. The newspapers carried the account of a former lumberjack who started climbing Mt. Fuji every year when he was 89 and continued it until he was 100 (he may still be doing it, as far as I know). Mt. Fuji rises to 12,300 feet high. The centenarian climbed to the top wearing heavy socks but no shoes. The trek took him three days, with a couple of overnight stops in huts along the way. He made quite a party of the excursion, inviting along his fifty-year-old daughter and fifty-one-year-old friend, seven of his ten grandchildren, and three of his thirty-six grandchildren. A grand party!

The last time I hiked the Havasupi Canyon in our state, I was thinking to myself, "This *is* the last time." Each hike seems a little harder than the one before. This time, I went on down to the lower falls, a steep descent that has to be made by ladder part of the way — and back up by ladder as well. Panting and feeling sorry for myself as I made my laborious way up the ascent, I met an elderly English couple. In the course of our conversation I learned they were nearly eighty years old. They had just made the same trek — without complaint. In fact, with enthusiasm. It was at that moment I decided this would not be my last hike down the Havasupi Canyon. If they could do it at eighty, I could at fifty!

Old age is often more a state of mind than body. Joy and I were startled, when we were still in our twenties, when friends our age said of their newly finished home, "This is our retirement house. We plan to live here 'til we die." Mid-twenties, and already "settling down." We couldn't conceive of such a thing.

Since then I have known many people who started practicing for their old age when they were in their twenties and thirties. By the time they reached middle age, they were good at being old. Since old age is inevitable, we do need to get ready — but not by practicing, not by trying to stamp out change, but by learning to walk with confidence in God while seeking first His kingdom and His righteousness.

I must confess that even now I'm beginning to experience one common element of older age — the slipping memory. Even that can be managed, however, so long as your sense of humor holds out! President Reagan used to love to tell the story of an old couple just slightly more advanced in memory loss than I am. They were getting ready for bed when she said, "Oh, I just am so hungry for ice cream and there isn't any in the house."

The old man said, "I'll go get you some."

She said, "That's good. Vanilla. Vanilla with chocolate sauce."

"Vanilla with chocolate sauce," he said.

"And whipped cream on top."

And he said, "Whipped cream on top."

"And a cherry."

"And a cherry on top."

"Please write it down," she said. "I know you'll forget. Vanilla with chocolate sauce, whipped cream, and a cherry."

"I don't need to write it down, I won't forget that — vanilla with chocolate sauce with whipped cream with a cherry on top."

Away he went. After a little while he came back and handed her a paper bag. She opened it and took out a ham sandwich.

"I told you to write it down," she said. "You forgot the mustard."

Joy and I love the story. We identify with it. Already we are creeping upward toward the age of unreliable memories. We know, we have had to face up to the fact, that with just a few more years we, too, will enter into that future called old age. We aren't frightened, though, because we know something else.

## It Holds God

The God of Abraham and Isaac and Jacob, the God of yesterday, is also the God of tomorrow. He is already there, ahead of us, inviting us into a future with Him. Notice the tone of assurance in these scriptures:

> Through him [Jesus] you believe in God, who raised him from the dead and glorified him, and so your faith and hope are in God (I Peter 1:21).
>
> Paul, an apostle of Christ Jesus by the command of God our Savior and of Christ Jesus our hope . . . (I Tim. 1:1).
>
> Now faith is being sure of what we hope for and certain of what we do not see (Heb. 11:1).

These scriptures (and so many more) are hopeful. They remind us of that wonderful hymn, "My hope is built on nothing less than Jesus' blood and righteousness." Our hope is in the Lord — not in an ageless body or even in the power of positive thinking. In Him we trust. In our relationship with Him is our joy and confidence.

Paradoxically, much of our confidence that we can handle the future stems from admitting we aren't handling the present. We have in a sense given up. We no longer try to run things, or people. Our hope is not in ruling the world, but in submitting to the One who does, the God above all Gods. Our rebellion is over; we no longer have to do it "my way." We are, indeed, changing the things we can change and accepting the things we can't. We have finally gained enough wisdom to know the difference. We now let Him who was, is, and is to come be in charge. We live longingly toward Him whom we must face, who will one day judge, and who will either welcome us into our eternal reward or will allow to go to the consequences we have chosen. He is God. We trust in Him.

## Therefore It Holds Hope

Those who believe in Him have hope; they face their future without fear. Billy Graham tells the story of Jack Moudy, a former military helicopter pilot. One Christmas his wife, Lois and a couple of her friends planned a special present for their husbands and fiancee. They gave them a hot air balloon ride, an experience Lois knew Jack had always wanted. Arrangements were made for December 15, a bright, clear Florida day.

After the excitement surrounding the lift-off of the balloon, the women followed it in their car. The balloon was sailing low, so the women could hear the men singing Christmas carols to the residents below. Somehow in their excitement, they didn't see the high tension wire that snared the balloon and gondola. In a split second what had been a moment of joy and of celebration turned to tragedy as the men, one by one, leaped from the basket to their death below.

Billy Graham invited Lois to speak at one of his crusades. She told the crowd she knew Jack's consuming hope when he jumped was that he could survive. But if he didn't she knew he was convinced he would be in heaven with the Lord. Then she added, "I know tonight, that if I were to die even this very night, I, too, would be in heaven with the Lord, and with Jack. That total assurance wasn't always there for Jack and me. I was fortunate enough to have transferred my trust from myself to Jesus Christ at the age of thirteen. . . . Since Jack's death, my own life has changed dramatically. And I think I'd have to say the biggest change has been a really supernatural peace and absence of anxiousness. I still worry and have times of apprehension, but in no way like I used to. And I believe that I have this peace because I've been able to see firsthand that the Lord really meets us in our times of need. Although the pain of missing Jack is very real, the comforting presence of the Lord is very real also."[5]

Peace, because of the presence of the Lord.
Hope, because of trust in the Lord.
No matter what the future holds.

If you were to die today, do you know you'd go to heaven? As you think about the future, are you preoccupied with whether you have adequate insurance, adequate security? Are you anxious about tomorrow? You don't have to be. You can count on it — there will be trouble tomorrow, you'll have some heartaches, your body will continue to deteriorate, old age with its attending complications are inescapable, unless you die first. But look further, will you? Look past old age to eternity. Are you ready for that? Is everything well between you and the Lord? Can you sing that song, "It is well, it is well with my soul"? Have you found a peace that passes understanding? Or when you look to the future are you uptight and nervous?

What is your hope?

No, the question should be, "Who is your hope?"

Ecclesiastes 3:1-8
Matthew 6:25-34
I Timothy 1:1
Hebrews 11:1
I Peter 1:21

**Endnotes**

**1.** Each of these incorrect predictions taken from "Never Say Never," *Science 84*, January/February 1984, p. 39.

**2.** Robert Browning, "Rabbi ben Ezra."

**3.** "Sailing to Byzantium"

**4.** Mesa *Tribune*, May 10, 1987, co. Tribune Media Services, Inc., 1987.

**5.** *Till Armageddon*. Waco, Texas: Word Books, co. 1981, p.56

# 8
# Is There Life After Death?

"If a man dies," wonders the suffering Job, speaking for all of humanity, "will he live again?" (Job. 14:14). To this question the Bible answers unequivocally, "Yes."

Who hasn't memorized these words form the twenty-third Psalm, the most frequently requested scripture at funeral services.

> Even though I walk
> through the valley of the shadow of death,
> I will fear no evil,
> for you are with me;
> Your rod and your staff,
> they comfort me. . . .
> Surely goodness and love will follow me
> all the days of my life,
> And I will dwell in the house of the Lord forever
> (Psa. 23:4-6).

Second in popularity only to Psalm 23 are these words of Jesus:

> Do not let your heart be troubled. Trust in God; trust also in me. In my Father's house are many rooms; if it were not so, I would have told you. I am going to prepare a place for you. And if I go and prepare a place for you, I will come back and take you to be with me that you also may be where I am. You know the way to the place where I am going (John 14:1-4).

A few years ago Francis Shaffer published a much-discussed book, *How Shall We Then Live*? His provocative title (in light of the grace of God, how *shall* we live?) hints at a similar question: *How shall we then die?* Can we ask the one question apart from the other? How we choose to live affects our manner of dying, and how we choose to die affects our manner of living. We live, in fact, with this inescapable, intrusive question. Our decisions, our values, our relations — everything we do and are is colored by the stance we assume toward death. Is it final? Is it transitional? Is there more to my personal existence than what can be experienced through my physical senses? I'm aware of here and now; will I also have awareness there and then?

How shall we then face our dying?

## With Dread or Denial?

Flying to Phoenix I came across an article in the plane's magazine entitled "Oceans Apart," a rather humorous comparison of the typical Brit and American. The writer, assuming a decidedly British point of view, handles us Americans rather roughly. One of her points rings true, however:

> The single most important thing to know about Americans

> — the attitude that *truly* distinguishes them from the British and explains much superficially odd behavior — is that *Americans think that death is optional.* They may not admit it, and will probably laugh if it's suggested; but it's a state of mind — a kind of national leitmotiv if you like — that colors everything they do. "I'm Gonna Live Forever" is the unofficial national anthem. There's a nagging suspicion that you can delay death or (who knows, avoid it altogether) if you really try. This explains the common preoccupation with health, aerobics, plastic surgery, and education.[1]

What do you think? Is she treating us fairly? Do we Americans really think we're going to live an earthly, flesh and blood existence forever? I doubt it. Ms. Walmsley exaggerates in service of truth, though, doesn't she? When you observe the fear with which many Americans approach the dying or even the subject of death, you can't deny her accusation too vigorously.[2]

Dr. Roy MacGregor, who advises doctors on the care and treatment of the desperately ill, believes modern medical care is extending the dying process rather than prolonging life.

> Both doctors and patients are losing their sensitivity to the inevitability and the appropriateness of death in certain circumstances. . . . Is respiration failing? Use the respirator. Have the kidneys stopped working? Start dialysis. Slowly and sadly our attitude is becoming: "If we have the technical capability, we must always use it."[3]

So the dying is extended, but the quality of life is not improved. Preferring what they take little pleasure in to what they have little knowledge of, some people will submit to any medical treatment if it promises to delay the inevitable.

A good measure of our national paranoia on the subject was the chorus of outrage at Colorado Governor Lamb's reported comment that "the elderly have a duty to die." That's not exactly what the governor said, but it's what people though he said. The misquotation stirred up so much controversy he had to write the media to set the record straight. Of course, his correction didn't make the headlines. The damage was done.

> "I never said the elderly have a duty to die," he insisted. "I said, '*We* all have a duty to die.' It was the Denver *Post* that changed the 'we' to 'you' and added the elderly and terminally ill, to whom I had not referred in my speech."[4]

Actually, I have never though of dying as a duty, an option one could chose or refuse, but the governor was onto something, wasn't he? At the very least, he was trying to force an unwilling public to recognize life's transitoriness. The truth is, we are all terminal! "A man is destined to die once, and after that to face judgment . . ." (Heb. 9:27).

Yet with what dread, with what denial, some people refuse to face the fact. One of England's leading philosophers in the nineteenth century was Jeremy Bentham. From such a sage one might expect a word of wisdom on the subject of life after death. Instead, his is the supreme example of the absurdity of denial. He died a quite wealthy man, bequeathing his entire estate to a London hospital — but the will contained a proviso: his dried skeleton should be dressed in a business suit, topped with a death mask and his old hat, placed on a small movable platform, and at every board meeting wheeled into the board room and sat at the head of the table. For over 100 years the official minutes of the meetings of the board of that London hospital had this line in it: "Jeremy Bentham present but not voting."[5]

Bentham's antic reminds me of a couple of lines from a poem by Dylan Thomas, written on the death of his father:

> Do not go gentle into that good night.
> Rage, rage against the night.

But raging, or cursing, or dreading, or denying won't banish death. There's a healthier attitude.

## With Acceptance of the Inevitable

One of the Bible's virtues is its realism. It neither hides death's certainty nor denies its force. It doesn't romanticize, either. "The last *enemy* to be destroyed is death" (I Cor. 15:26). Yet being in the Lord overcomes fear of the inevitable, for all of life (including death) is seen from God's perspective. His is the bigger picture, including not only life and death but also life after death.

As I recall, I first began thinking seriously about death's proper place in the scheme of things one day when I was walking among the magnificent Douglas firs in a Pacific Northwest forest. I'd never paid much attention to the cycles of nature. Oh, I had survived biology class as a high school sophomore, but I hadn't applied much of my book-learning to my everyday experience. On this particular excursion, however, with my mind preoccupied by some problem unrelated to my beautiful surroundings, suddenly for the first time I looked at something I had been familiar with all my life but had never really seen. Scattered here and there among the firs and pines and deciduous trees and underbrush were fallen trees, lying across my path like rotting, vermin-infested carcasses. Even the giant Douglas fir could not live forever. It died, its remains fertilizing the soil for a new generation.

Please forgive me for belaboring the obvious here. Why I suddenly saw with such force something so commonplace, why I hadn't thought of this before, I can't explain, unless I was only then able to see my future in the crumbling giants. They were once but seeds, then flourishing saplings, and finally mature plants stretching straight and tall toward the heavens. Then one day they sickened and died.

Trees do that. People do, too. So the Psalmist justly asks,

> What man can live and not see death,
> or save himself from the power of the grave? (Psa. 89:48).

Facing death seems to be more of a problem for our affluent society than it is in the poorer countries I have visited. There I have sensed a more realistic, a more honest viewpoint. Death occurs more frequently among infants and children. And when the elderly die, they don't expire somewhere else, in a hospital or nursing home, hiding their offense. They die at home, in the presence of their families. They can't afford the luxury of anything else. As a result, their little ones are not shielded from the shock of sudden final departures. They see the last breath, hear its gasp. Then too, unlike this naive city pastor walking in the woods one day, they live closer to nature; they see the young sprouts springing out of the forest's fallen.

There really is something spiritual in this analogy, isn't there, something very like the Biblical view of death and life? It teaches that we, too, began as a seed and sprouted into children (even our language suggests the comparison — for we affectionately call our little ones "young sprouts," don't we?), then adolescents and mature adults. But we are destined one day to die.

When its reality finally hits us, that's when we demand to know: when a man dies, *will he live again*? There's nothing merely academic about our inquiry. We ask urgently and we ask personally: When I die and my remains are lowered into the ground, is that the end of me? All my strivings to become something, all the struggles of God and my loved ones to make something of me, were they all in vain? After death, is there nothing? Dare I hope for more, an extension of some kind? Isn't it possible this person, this I, can somehow transcend the grave, can throw off flesh and blood and bone and sinew and still *be*?

The Bible not only admits the possibiltiy, but promises it.

So how then shall we face our dying?

## As A Reflection of Our Living

I've not heard of many genuine deathbed conversions. Perhaps if we knew exactly when we were going to die, we could live without God until just the last moment, then repent and claim faith in Him. Perhaps, but I doubt we would do it. Fortunately Augustine lived long enough to make good on his youthful prayer ("Lord, deliver me from sin, but not yet"), but that delayed petition would lead most of us to keep on sinning beyond the point of no return. People die the way they have lived. If they fought against or ignored God in their living, they'll fight or ignore Him in their dying. If they lived in His daily presence, they die assured that he is — and will be always — with them. They offer proof for the maxim, "As we grow older, we don't change; we just become more of the same."

As far as we know, only human beings are conscious of their coming deaths. This consciousness gives us a decided advantage over other living beings, because we have a chance of turning our foreknowledge to gain, enhancing the days we do have, choosing life-enriching and life-prolonging options, preparing ourselves for the approaching transition, and composing ourselves to die with befitting dignity. Even with the "intimations of mortality" we are granted, however, only the spiritually sensitive succeed in preparing to die well. The truth is, we die as we have lived.

## With Anticipation

There's a little more to be said about the Bible's unblinking view of death. Scripture presents our passing as conclusion and beginning. Jesus speaks of both when he comforts his friends Mary and Martha, whose brother Lazarus has died.

> I am the resurrection and the life. He who believes in me will live, even though he dies; and whoever lives and believes in me will never die (John 11:25).

His words recall the lines we have already read in Psalm 23:

> Even though I walk
>   through the valley of the shadow of death
> I will fear no evil,
>   for you are with me;
> Your rod and your staff,
>   they comfort me. . . .
> and I will dwell in the house of the Lord forever.

Right now, the Psalmist asserts, even in the most trying of circumstances, I am enjoying the presence of the Lord. I am not alone. And then, in the shadow of death, I am enjoying the presence of the Lord. Dread yields to anticipation, denial to affirmation. Doubt flees and confidence abides. Yes, yes there is life after death, and I'm looking forward to it. "I will dwell . . ."

The late Christian columnist Joseph Bayly, has written about death with rare authority. Three times he went to the cemetery to bury a son. One died in infancy, another as a child, and the third in promising young manhood. The grieving father stood before a standing-room-only crowd at his grown son's service. What can a father say at such a moment? How does he express the anguish in his heart? With trembling voice Joe Bayly spoke out of the depths of his grief. "I have come to talk to you about my earthly son and our Heavenly Father."[6]

That one sentence sums it up, doesn't it? We have a Father whose love embraces earth and heaven, life and death, and life after death. He walks with us now. He waits for us there. As we love our children, with such a love (to the power of infinity) He loves us. What we can't do, however, He can. Nothing can separate God's loved ones from Him (Rom. 8:38-39).

Some time ago my friend Linda Carlson gave me this lovely poem by Nancy Wood, an Indian. I might not have treasured it so highly except for an experience I want to tell you about.

> Today is a very good day to die
> Every living thing is in harmony with me
> Every voice sings a chorus within me
> All beauty has come to rest in my eyes
> All bad thoughts have departed from me

Today is a very good day to die
My land is peaceful around me
My fields have been turned the last time
My child has come home
Yes, today is a very good time to die.

Because of the circumstances surrounding my loss of my father, I appreciate this little poem — and I believe that for dying some days are better than others.

One evening as Joy and I were reading in bed, the phone rang. I answered. The voice was Dad's; he'd called just to chat. That in itself was a little surprising, because in our family we almost never telephoned just to talk. We seem to need "a reason." On this occasion, though, Dad had nothing else on his agenda. He merely wanted to talk, as if that were important enough in itself.

The next morning my secretary broke into an appointment in my study to tell me Joy was on the line. I knew it had to be urgent, for Joy doesn't interrupt me except in an emergency. When I picked up the telephone, she said, "Your Dad died this morning." It was a heart attack.

I caught the first plane to Las Vegas, then rented a car to drive the additional miles to Pahrump. At first I didn't notice anything unusual, but after comforting my stepmother I began checking out their five-acre place. I saw something that I had never seen before. Everything was in order. All Dad's projects were completed. The tools were in their proper places. Nothing was unfinished.

You'd have to know my Dad to appreciate what I'm saying. Dad was a putterer-extraordinaire, a first class fixer-upper and tear-aparter. He always worked on several projects at a time. Give him a little time and he could transform any acreage into a congenial junk yard, every piece having its purpose and eventual place. That day, the yard, the toolshed, the other buildings were immaculate.

Later, when I began going through his business affairs with my stepmother, we discoverd all his paperwork in order. Then I understood why he had called the night before. I'm not saying he knew he was going to die; I just knew he was ready. He had taken care of his relationship with the Lord a long time ago. No problem there. But everything else was in readiness, also. Dad could have written the poem. For him then, "Today is a Very Good Day to Die."

The Apostle Paul was also ready.

> For me to live is Christ and to die is gain. If I am to go on living in the body, this will mean fruitful labor for me. Yet what shall I choose? I do not know! I am torn between the two: I desire to depart and be with Christ, which is better by far; but it is more necessary for you that I remain in the body (Phil. 1:21-24).

He was a prisoner, not knowing whether he would be acquitted and released or convicted and condemned to die. If death should be his fate, he was prepared. "Today is a good day to die." It's also a good day to live, if that should be God's will.

Jesus had the same assurance on the cross. "Father, into your hands I commit my spirit" (Luke 23:46). He was both reaffirming His trust in His father, with whom He had been as one throughout His ministry, and looking to His Father to carry Him through the transition He was about to make from life to death. He knew His future was brighter than anything earth had to offer.

Jesus had been getting ready for that moment throughout His life. Again and again He had alerted His disciples to his coming death. No one could take life from

Him, He insisted. He was giving it up. Even Pilate would have been helpless to condemn Him without receiving permission from above (John 19:11). He was leaving His work here to enter His kingdom beyond (John 18:36). It was to this end He had been preparing Himself.

We also want to get ready. In an earlier chapter we studied Matthew 24 and 25, in which Jesus speaks earnestly with His disciples about living in anticipation of the end of the world. The alert needs to be sounded again, doesn't it? We don't want to be caught unawares.

In Denver, Colorado in the 1950's a six-year-old boy dying of cancer expressed a wish to see the President of the United States, who was in Denver at the time. One of President Eisenhower's aides told him about this little guy's wish, and Ike spontaneously decided to grant it. Imagine the buzzing in the neighborhood when the President's black limousine pulled up in front of little Paul's house. Ike knocked and Paul's father opened it, obviously surprised. Donald Haley was dressed in his old jeans and dirty T-shirt. His hair was unkempt and his beard unshaven. Right behind him was little Paul, all eyes.

"Paul, I understand you wanted to see me. I'm glad to see you." The little guy took the president's hand and Ike led him back down the sidewalk to see the big, black limousine — something neither Paul nor any of his neighbors had ever seen before. The President chatted with him awhile, then put out his hand again and said goodbye and drove off.

For a long time to come, Paul and his family and his neighbors talked about the day the President of the United States came to see him. Everybody remembered it with gladness except for one man — Donald Haley. Each time anybody brought it up, he kept saying, "Those jeans, the old shirt, the unshaven face — what a way to meet the President of the United States.''[7]

One of these days you're going to meet face to face Someone far more important than the President of the United States. Are you looking forward to the meeting? Are you ready?

Job 14:14
Psalm 10:10; 23:4,6; 89:48
Luke 23:46
John 11:25; 14:1-4; 18:36; 19:11
Romans 8:38-39
I Corinthians 15:26
Philippians 1:21-24
Hebrews 9:27

**Endnotes**

**1.** Jane Walmsley, *TWA Ambassador*, July 1987, p. 13.

**2.** Some of our jokes play on an American's discomfort when the subject is introduced. One of my favorites is about the fellow who met an old friend of many years and as they chatted asked, ''How's the wife?'' The guy said, ''She's in heaven.'' ''Oh,'' the first fellow said, ''I'm so sorry.'' Then he realized that didn't sound too good so he said, ''No, no, I mean I'm not glad.'' Well, that didn't sound good either. Finally he said, ''What I mean is, I'm so surprised.''

**3.** ''The Inevitability of Death,'' *Christianity Today,* March 6, 1987, p. 24.

**4.** *Time*, May 14, 1984.

**5.** Margaret T. Applegarth, *Twelve Baskets Full.* New York: Harper and Brothers, co. 1947, p. 74.

**6.** Quoted by Dr. C. Everett Koop, U.S. Surgeon General, in ''Out of Our Hearts,'' *Eternity*, October 1986, p. 72.

**7.** Quoted in Charles R. Swindoll, *Growing Deep in the Christian Life,* Portland: Multnomah Press, co. 1986, pp. 293-294.

# 9

# What Is Heaven Like?

What is heaven like? No one ever worked out a more elaborate and demanding answer to the question than the ancient Egyptians. Their well-designed post-earth existence was an extension of earthly life; this life was to be spent preparing for the next. The wealthy, especially, were concerned to make adequate provision so they could always and forever live at the level to which they had become accustomed here. Their greatest fear was of somehow not making the proper transition from one life to the next and , once having made it, of going hungry or thirsty or unclothed. They prepared a tomb as their eternal resting place, equipping it with ample food and furnishing for their everlasting ease.

They preserved a record of their earthly accomplishments on the tomb's walls, had their bodies mummified and had placed in the tomb papyrus scrolls containing various magic formulas. Archaeologists have even found pictures on the walls depicting boating on the Nile, picnicking with relatives and friends, enjoying good wine in a cool garden. Admittedly, they wouldn't have to do a great deal for themselves, since their earthly servants would still be on the job in the afterlife, a prospect which must have been less than thrilling to them.[1]

If you were to visit Egypt today, you would of course include some of these famous tombs on your itinerary, at the very least taking in the great pyramids. You wouldn't be able to examine the treasures buried there; human scavangers made off with them a long time ago. You would still be impressed, though, with the tremendous energy these ancients expended on life after death in order to be certain it would be more of the same.

## It's Like New

The Bible's most familiar description of heaven paints a far different picture. Revelation 21 promises that nothing will be the same. Heaven will be like new:

a new heaven
a new earth
a new Jerusalem
a new bride
"I am making everything new."

You'll find most Christians, unlike the ancient Egyptians, pretty complacent about burial practices. We don't construct tombs and furnish them; when we die, we're going to something entirely new. A mummified body will be of no use; we're getting one far better suited to our new environment (I Cor. 15:42-54; II Cor. 5:1-4). We won't need this old body any more.

## It's Like A Perfect Marriage

More important than the resurrection body will be the everlasting relationship with the Lord. It will be like the freshness and excitement of a perfect new marriage.

> I saw the Holy City, the new Jerusalem, coming down out of heaven from God, prepared as a bride beautifully dressed for her husband (Rev. 21:2).

You have to have a pretty good imagination to see this picture. A city becomes a bride. That sounds like some kind of surrealistic dream, with one image warping and wrapping into another far different one. The city is a place to dwell; the bride is a person with whom to dwell. Imagine the best marriage in the finest place on earth. Heaven offers even better.

In all the Book of Revelation, the core concern is the believers' relationship with the Lord. For example, read Revelation 19:6-9, where the marriage of the bride (the church) and the Lamb (Christ) is celebrated in heaven. In this book the Lamb always symbolizes purity and innocence, or the Pure and Innocent Person (Jesus). This, then is a picture of perfection: One who has been purified — the bride — is married to the only naturally pure one. Purity and innocence meet the Pure and Innocent Person (see Revelation 21:9-14). Heaven is a gathering of persons deemed perfect through the blood of Jesus Christ. These persons, collectively the Body of Christ, the Household of God, the Assembly of God, the New Jerusalem (among other metaphors), are here named cumulatively the Bride of Christ. Heaven, then, is the holy God and His holy people enjoying each other's company forever.

The emphasis is on "enjoying." Irish playwright

George Bernard Shaw, in his play *Man and Superman* takes a more cynical view of heaven (although he's not denigrating heaven so much as satirizing the British, something Shaw never tires of doing). Having already called heaven "the most angelically dull place in all creation," the statute speaks further on the subject:

> At every one of those concerts in England you will find rows of weary people who are there, not because they really like classical music, but because they think they ought to like it. Well, there is the same thing in heaven. A number of people sit there in glory, not because they're happy, but because they think they owe it to their position to be there. They are almost all English.[2]

Shaw's humor is delightful; his theology is abominable. He's left out the most important part of the story. He doesn't mention the bridegroom! The bride isn't the only one who chooses the marriage; the groom also desires the bride (see Eph. 5:21-27). People who enjoy arguing over who will or will not be in heaven usually leave out an important teaching on which the Bible is very clear. The inhabitants of heaven are those whom the groom has chosen and who have chosen Him. A perfect marriage is one in which both partners want each other, love each other, and determine to remain with each other as long as they possibly can. So it is in heaven.

What are the qualities, then, of this perfect marriage? Many ingredients are required in an ideal match. Let me name a few.

*Compatibility.* This encompassing word points to similarity in values and a meshing of personalities. The two persons remain distinct individuals, but they complement rather than compete with one another.

*Trust.* Without it, there's no relationship.

*Pleasure in each other's company.* The husband and wife just enjoy being together. For no particular reason, either. They don't have to talk, don't have to do anything. If you were to take a trip with Joy and me somewhere across the country, you might even wonder whether we are getting along. We often drive for miles, maybe hundreds of miles, without speaking. But if you would ask us, "Are you upset with one another?" we would be surprised. To the contrary. We just enjoy being together. There's a sweet communion deeper than words or activities.

*Mutual help.* This hardly needs to be said, does it? Each enjoys helping and bringing out the best in the other.

*Tenderness.* Gone is all hint of machoism, all boasting or bullying or nagging.

*Growth.* One of my greatest pleasures in marriage has been watching Joy grow, discovering additional dimensions to her being that I was totally unaware of in our early years of marriage. It has been like receiving a long series of unanticipated bonuses.

*Service.* This word seldom appears in lists like this one, but I think it's essential. The best marriages I know anything about are those in which the husband and wife have dedicated themselves to persons and causes beyond their home. Jesus said, "It is more blessed to give than to receive" (Acts 20:35).

Mix all these ingredients together and you get a little of heaven on earth. Of course, there are many others that could be added to this recipe, but these are enough as a reminder of just how good marriage — and heaven — can be.

By now it should be pretty evident why we need to prepare now for heaven. If we want to live with the Lord forever, then we must be actively making our relationship more compatible now. This entails learning to trust Him, to enjoy His company, to do what he wants us to do, to love tenderly as He loves, to serve others as He has demonstrated — now. All this is groundwork for the joy to come, like the engagement before a perfect marriage.

## What Else Is Heaven Like?

*It's Like Inheriting Everything You've Always Wanted.*
It is exchanging your wheelchair for a liberated body.
It is not being hungry anymore.
It is not having the pressures of your high-tension job any more.
It is not having any more emotional traumas to endure.
It is being accepted and wanted.
It is being free from addiction.
It is living without war any more.
It is overcoming sin forever.
It is all this and more.

What do you really want in life? Although we are often too timid to say so in public, a surprisingly high percentage of us would answer,

"I want to be with God."
*"The dwelling of God is with men."*
"I want to be loved."
*"God Himself will be with them and be their God.*
"I want to be free of this pain and sorrow."
*"He will wipe every tear from their eyes" (see also Isaiah 25:8).*

"I don't want to be afraid of death anymore."

> *"There will be no more death or mourning or crying or pain."*

"I want to live, I want to go for the gusto, I want more!"

> *"To him who is thirsty I will give to drink without cost from the spring of the water of life."*

"I want to make my parents proud of me." (We never outgrow this deep desire to please our parents, to make them feel we turned out okay.)

> *"I will be his God and he will be my son."*

We could summarize all these desires (and the many more we have) in one phrase: *We want to live victoriously.* Revelation presents heaven as the haven of the survivors, victorious in life's struggles, faithful to their mission, having stayed the course and earned the winner's laurels. It is to win this victory that Paul urges us to

> . . . stand firm. Let nothing move you. Always give yourselves fully to the work of the Lord, because you know that your labor in the Lord is not in vain (I Cor. 15:58).

A great victory it is, too. Paul argues throughout I Corinthians 15 for the true and essential nature of Christ's resurrection. With these ringing words he brings his argument to a climax:

> For the perishable must clothe itself with the imperishable, and the mortal with immortality. When the perishable has been clothed with the imperishable, and the mortal with immortality, then the saying that is written will come true: "Death has been swallowed up in victory."
> "Where, O death, is your victory?"

> "Where, O death, is your sting?"
> The sting of death is sin, and the power of sin is the law.
> But thanks be to God! He gives us the victory through our Lord Jesus Christ.

Do you see? If we "hang in there" with the Lord, He will hang onto us as well. Then everything He has promised will become ours.

So heaven is: 1. where everything is new, 2. where you will enjoy a close, secure, and everlasting relationship with your Lord, and 3. where we reach the very heights of personal victorious living. You cannot be defeated when you are in Him.

One more matter demands attention, however. Sentimental, well-intentioned folks stubbornly insist, "Everybody's going to heaven when they die. They're just going by different routes. All roads lead to heaven." That sounds so good, so comforting. But it's so wrong.

All this talk about heaven is incomplete if we don't point out the obverse side:

> But the cowardly, the unbelieving, the vile, the murderers, the sexually immoral, those who practice magic arts, the idolaters, and all liars — their place will be in the fiery lake of burning sulfur (Rev. 21:8).

Why such a dread destiny? Because God hates them? No, because they chose to marry someone else. Having declined His invitation to be His bride, they cannot expect the bliss that life with Him will be. By comparison with such a life, anything else would be hell indeed, a hell really of their own creating, since they wanted to be their own gods.

This isn't the only such list in the Bible. Here is a very specific one from the Apostle Paul:

> Furthermore, since they did not think it worthwhile to retain the knowledge of God, he gave them over to a depraved mind, to do what ought not to be done. They have become filled with every kind of wickedness, evil, greed and depravity. They are full of envy, murder, strife, deceit and malice. They are gossips, slanderers, God-haters, insolent, arrogant and boastful; they invent ways of doing evil; they disobey their parents; they are senseless, faithless, heartless, ruthless. Although they know God's righteous decree that those who do such things deserve death, they not only continue to do these very things but also approve of those who practice them (Rom. 1:28-32).

So they must face the consequences of their choices. God "gives them up" to what they want. They have spurned His wooing.

When I was courting Joy, the moment came for me to ask her to be my wife. My good friend Herb (already married and therefore an expert on these matters) and I went shopping, bought a ring, and planned how I would give it to her. At the appointed hour Joy and I drove up to Skinner's Butte, a romantic spot overlooking Eugene, Oregon. It was just the right setting on a beautiful evening. From nowhere I just casually brought forth the ring, made my little speech, and placed it on her finger. I remember how intensely I wanted to hear her say "Yes." Which she did. In so many ways, that moment was the beginning of the rest of my life! But what if she had refused? What would I have done to her?

Well, for a starter, you can be certain I'd have made another speech! But that's about all. Would I have beat her? No. Would I have reviled her? No. Would I have thought less of her? (Well, I suppose I would have questioned her judgment!) You know what would have happened. She would have gone her way and I would have gone mine. The relationship would have been over, but not of my choosing. I would have had to accept the consequences of her refusal.

Heaven is for the people who have accepted God's proposal. They want to be married to Him forever. Those who reject Him He simply gives up to what they want. The picture of their lot is so gruesome because by comparison existence apart from God is ugly. Even on earth it is no pleasure to dwell in the midst of godless people, who live and breathe only for themselves. They are the best argument there is for wanting to be married to God.

Friedrich Nietzsche once exclaimed, "There is an old illusion — it is called good and evil."[3] Sorry, Mr. Nietzsche, it is not an illusion. It's a reality, and it forces a choice with consequences immediate and eternal. Nothing distinguishes the social repercussions more sharply than Paul's discussion of the fruit of the Spirit and the acts of the sinful nature (Gal. 5:16-26). Imagine a social group totally devoted to,

> . . . sexual immorality, impurity, and debauchery; idolatry and witchcraft; hatred, discord, jealousy, fits of rage, selfish ambition, dissensions, factions and envy; drunkenness, orgies, and the like.

How can such people expect to dwell in heaven, which will be governed by the Spirit of God? (As a matter of fact, it's difficult to imagine such people being governed at all, isn't it? One can only picture them in anarchy, which could perhaps be a synonym for hell.) You have no trouble imagining a heaven peopled with souls whose character is dominated by "love, joy, peace, patience, kindness, goodness, faithfulness, gentleness and self-control," though, do you?

It isn't really very hard to elect which group to fall in with, is it? Heaven and hell are plainly foreshadowed on earth. What sometimes discourages us, though, is evil's strength. Wrong so often seems to be winning and righteousness so seldom is rewarded. Don't give up. When you become discouraged, remember this little story from Ray Stedman. It has helped me on more than one dark day. It's about an elderly missionary couple returning to New York City after forty years of faithful service in Africa. They returned without pension or income or friends in their homeland. Their health was broken and their discouraged spirits were nearly so.

Aboard their steamship was Theodore Roosevelt, arriving back home from one of his hunting expeditions. Attention and fanfare accompained the former president across the ocean; isolation and loneliness attended the missionaries. The old man was resentful, complaining to his wife. "It's just not fair. Why should we have given our lives in faithful service to God in Africa all these many years and have no one care a thing about us? Here this man comes back from a hunting trip and everybody makes much over him, but nobody gives two hoots about us."

"Dear, you shouldn't feel that way," she soothed him.

When they docked in New York, Roosevelt was greeted by a band, the mayor and other political dignitaries. No one noticed the missionary couple as they slipped off the ship and located a cheap apartment on the East Side, hoping to find work the next day.

Forty years they had served, and nobody noticed.

That evening, the old man exploded. "I can't take this; God is not treating us fairly."

"Why don't you go in the bedroom and tell that to the Lord?" his wise wife counselled.

He did. When he returned she saw in his face that he was a new man.

"The Lord settled it with me," he said. "I told him how bitter I was that the President should receive this tremendous homecoming, when no one met us as we returned home. And when I finished, it seemed as though the Lord put his hand on my shoulder and simply said, *'But you're not home yet!'* "[4]

So we await our homecoming. In the meantime we sing,

> This world is not my home,
> I'm just a-passing through;
> My treasures are laid up
> Somewhere beyond the blue.
> The angels beckon me from heaven's open door
> And I can't feel at home in this world anymore.

Since we don't have a permanent address on planet earth, we don't expect full pay here. That will come when we get home.

Revelations 19:6-9; 21:1-11
Ephesians 5:21-27
Romans 1:28-32
I Corinthians 15:42-58
Isaiah 25:8

**Endnotes**

**1.** Chaim Potok, *Wanderings*, New York: Fawcett Crest, co. 1978, pp. 66-67.

**2.** Act III. *Complete Plays with Prefaces*, Volume III. New York: Dodd, Mead and Company, 1963, pp. 613, 615.

**3.** From "Old and New Tables"

**4.** Condensed from *Talking to my Father*, excerpted in *Leadership*, Summer 1987, p. 48.

# 10

# How Can I Be A Better Person?

Many of the questions in this book have been about tomorrow: end times, life after death, the nature of heaven. In each chapter the scriptures we studied urged us to get ready for the future. This final chapter is a most appropriate conclusion to those inquiries. In view of what's coming, every serious Christian wants to know, "How can I get ready?" It's exactly the question II Peter 3:11 raises — and answers:

> Since everything will be destroyed in this way, what kind of people ought you to be? You ought to live holy and godly lives as you look forward to the day of God and speed its coming.

"Holy and glodly" are the scripture's words for people who are prepared for what's coming. They have become better persons.

How did they do it?

Take a trip to your neighborhood B. Dalton's or Walden's Book Store and you'll quickly find lots of advice for your personal improvement. This is not an exclusively Christian concern (although I think it's fair to say ours is a quest with a difference). Who in our generation doesn't talk about how to have a better life? Improving Americans' physical fitness is a multi-billion-dollar industry. Betterment of your mind, your finances, your social graces, your professional skills: for all these obsessions programs are available — for a modest fee, of course. The difference in the Christian's pursuit is in our model of perfection (Christ) and in the complete overhaul we desire. Our goal is nothing less than the transformation of the whole person, from inside out, mind, body, soul, emotions, relationships, morals, time and money management, a metamorphosis so radical it's accurately called being "born again."

I have the privilege of preaching to a host of these reborn persons every week. Bored with the banal and fed up with their mediocrity, they practice the disciplines of God's course for personal improvement. You actually see them growing better.

Most of them would be a little embarrassed to have II Peter's terms "godly" and "holy" applied to them. Godly and holy people never perceive these qualities in themselves, while people who believe they have achieved them, haven't. Suppose, though, you have decided you are ready to try for God's best for you. Do you know how to do it?

"Sure," you could easily tell me. "I have to become more and more like Christ."

Good answer. Go to it.

"Well," you might object, "I'm already trying, but it's

not all that easy. In fact, it almost seems the harder I try, the further I slip. I guess sainthood's just not for me!"

Yes it is. You're just going after it in the wrong way. Your aim is good. You could adopt no more noble goal than to become like Jesus, who was the godliest, holiest person who ever lived. You have correctly judged that you have only to decide one day you want to be like Him and then Presto, you are. It doesn't work that way.

So what should you do?

The best advice I could give would be to recommend a study of Ephesians 4:11-16. It's about growing up, into Christ. You'll find there that Christ has provided leaders for His church "to prepare God's people [that's you] for works of service" in order to build up the church [the people] until all "become mature [whole, perfect] attaining to the whole measure of the fullness of Christ." The apostle Paul challenges us to leave our childish ways behind and grow up into Christ. It's counsel for Christians who aren't satisfied to be only "born again." They want their new birth to lead to new growth, so they will no "longer be infants."

A ministerial colleague recently told a few of us the heartache their baby caused him and his wife. The infant lived only eight months, unable to grow to more than five pounds, and then was gone. He said sometimes as he held the tiny undeveloping body, he thought of how God must feel about spiritual babies who don't grow.

I wondered what it would be like if our bodies registered our spiritual as well as our chronological age. If our size were in proportion to our spiritual maturity, how big would we be? Some of us would look pretty grotesque, wouldn't we, shaking our rattles with wrinkled, liver-spotted hands? Aging spiritual infants — and even stillborns — are not rare, unfortunately. And they aren't pretty.

It has become popular in our country to boast of having been "born again." Americans like to talk about their religious experience, which is usually history. We should be challenged: "So you've been born again. So what? How much have you grown since your rebirth? Are you becoming a better person? What's your proof?"

My enthusiasm for ministry is constantly being recharged by men and women who really do want to grow. They're doing it and can prove it. From them as well as from God's Word I have picked up a few pointers on how to grow up in Christ. I'd like to pass them on to you.

**1. Admit you're not perfect yet.**

You haven't reached full maturity. Your exciting human potential is still to be realized. You have an adjustment to make here and there. Paul's charge to the Ephesians — and to us — rests on his premise that we are not yet all we ought to become. We must "grow up in every way. . . ."

Nobody makes me more ill at ease than a braggart self-righteously proclaiming his or her goodness. In one way or another, the message announces, "I live a good life and I am a good person. I am quite satisfied with who I am." I suspect my consciousness of my own failures makes me doubtful. Self-congratulations strike me as not only egotistical but as dishonest. They protest too much, reveal too little of the real person. A more objective appraisal declares, "There is no one righteous, not even one," for "all have sinned and fall short of the glory of God" (Rom. 3:10,23). I'm much more at ease with a confessed sinner who admits, "I am not yet what I want to become, but by the grace of God, I am on the way."

> If we claim to be without sin [when I call myself "good," isn't that what I am claiming?] we deceive ourselves and the truth is not in us. If we confess our sins, he is faithful and just and will forgive us our sins and purify us from all unrighteousness. If we claim we have not sinned, we make him out to be a liar and his word has no place in our lives (I John 1:8-10).

When the best-selling pop psychology book *I'm OK, You're OK* was first published, I read it eagerly. I liked the title and wanted to believe its promise. Upon reflection, the appealing slogan's emptiness became increasingly apparent. It seemed to offer a quick, altogether-too-easy route to an improved self-image (as if only the image and not the reality behind the image needed burnishing). If I can just convince myself I'm OK, the reasoning seemed to be, I'll like me better; and if I pre-judge you as OK, I'll like you better. Little more is required. (Of course, I'm grossly over-simplifying the book and doing an injustice to the writer, but I'm not unfairly caricaturing the way it has been popularly applied.)

I've finally concluded the title is not OK. It has misled and damaged people and reduces some otherwise valid teachings of transactional analysts to a simplistic slogan. People who announe their OKness are usually either self-deluded or bluffing. What's healthier is to admit I'm not OK and I'm dissatisfied with my imperfections, but I don't intend to stay in this shape. The Christian stance is balanced: As I am (on my own, without God), I'm not OK, and as you are without God, you're not OK, but that's OK, because by God's grace we are becoming OK.

The Bible doesn't play games with us; it calls a spade a spade, a sinner a sinner. Neither does it leave us forlorn, however. It promises salvation, that is, wholeness (complete OKness), through Jesus Christ. He came to the world not to condemn us, but to save us (John 3:16-17). His desire is blocked, though, by a braggart protesting his sufficiency. What can a Savior do for someone who rejects the rescue?

As for me, let me spend but an hour in the newspaper or watching TV news broadcasts and there's no way you could persuade me that any representative "you" is OK. If you're a typical human, there's something wrong with you individually because there's something terribly wrong with humanity generally. In addition, let me spend a little time reviewing my personal relationships, my job performance, my self-discipline, my deviant thought, and you'll find me equally unpersuaded that I'm OK. I haven't escaped the human blight, either. To be forced to believe that what I am and what your are is OK would drive me to despondency. Surely, we can be better than this. If this society is completely OK, what would a bad one look like?

As I've been saying, you can go to one extreme and brag, "I'm good, just as I am." There's no helping you if you do.

On the other hand, you can go to the other extreme and despair, "I'm no good at all. There's no hope for me." If you do, there still won't be any way to help you.

Thankfully, however, the person who believes in the God who designed and desires for us, who hasn't given up on us in spite of our rebellion against Him, enjoys a great hope. This person isn't trying to fool God or himself or anyone else. His hope is not in his "good self" but in his honesty and in God's graciousness.

**2. Admit you've got a struggle going on.**

Since God's grace is available, Paul can confidently urge the Ephesian Christians to grow up. They don't have to remain infants anymore. They'll have to struggle, of course, and the battle between the power of evil and the power of good won't be an easy one, but they won't be battling alone. And they will win.

I must be careful, lest I make this sound too easy, too certain. I'm thinking again of Job, who in the beginning was the epitome of moral, spiritual, financial, social, and familial success. He seemed better than better. He was the best; he had it all. Suddenly the bewildered Job's world collapsed. He lost everything: family, livestock, wealth, health. Everything. What should he do? Should he curse God and die? Should he hang on to his faith, even though that faith — or his God — seemed powerless to protect him from his losses? Or even worse, may have dictated his losses?

His plight elicits our sympathy, because we recognize his struggle as our own. Since we know the end of Job's story, we take comfort in identifying with him. Job neither abandons his faith nor curses God, and his faithfulness is rewarded. We hope to receive Job's reward even as we aspire to be as loyal and as honest as he, displaying his clear sense of values. He knew that

> To lose one's wealth is much
> To lose one's health is more
> To lose one's soul is such a loss
> That nothing can restore.

There's hope for the person who admits he's struggling; there's little hope, as we have already noted, for the person who fails to see his need to improve or, on the other hand, who gives up, insisting, "It's not worth it." Or, even worse, "I'm not worth it."

Don't quit. If you're worn out from defending yourself against Satan's attacks; if you are tormented by temptation, torn between right and wrong, tired of being tried but too tired to feel confident you can resist, then good for you. Admitting your condition may be your biggest asset right now. You are saying you haven't capitulated; you haven't cursed God. You still want to do better. You haven't let go of God and you don't want God to let go of you. You do need help, of course, but that help is available.

If you sometimes feel living the Christian life is like being at war, you aren't alone. That's exactly what it is.

> Finally, be strong in the Lord and in his mighty power. Put on the full armor of God so that you can take your stand against the devil's schemes. For our struggle is not against flesh and blood, but against the rulers, against the authorities, against the powers of this dark world and against the spiritual forces of evil in the heavenly realms. Therefore, put on the full armor of God . . . (Eph. 6:10-13).

Charles Swindoll's tale of the wasps provides one of the best symbols of this spiritual battle I have read. As a young lad his father took him along to his grandparents' South Texas cabin to open it up for a family reunion. As they were unlocking the door they knew they were in trouble when they saw the wasps between the window shade and the glass in the door. Chuck's stomach began to turn. (My feet would have been turning, I'm afraid — and running!)

They had a duty to do, so they had to forge ahead, on into a house filled with crawling, flying, buzzing wasps. Walls, ceilings, floors, light sockets, all covered with the pesky vermin. They didn't sting, because they were in their dormant stage. Their passivity allowed the Swindoll father and son to sweep them out by the thousands.

The job took all day. By bedtime Chuch fell exhausted onto his cot. But he kept hearing the buzzing of the wasps. His dad tried to convince him it was just his imagination, but the boy knew you don't feel your imagination under your head. Turning on the light, they flipped back the mattress and found — you guessed it — another whole layer of wasps. Would they never be free from these pesky, scary little beasts? (I once disturbed a hive of bees, and believe me, I had my hands full. The bees, by the way, weren't dormant, either! Just reading Swindoll's story made my flesh crawl.)[1]

When I read Paul's description of our spiritual battle against "spiritual forces of evil in the heavenly realms," I think of Chuck's buzzing, crawling, flying, pestering wasps, so hard to fight, so numerous, so repulsive, so bothersome, so ubiquitious, so unavoidable! Our struggle isn't against "flesh and blood." Would that it were. We would fight on even terms, then. But how do you fight ideas, influences, propaganda swarming all around you on the airwaves, in the subconscious, under your pillow? They're out to get you.

There's hope for people who acknowledge this fact. They are aware, for example, that they can not hang around the TV "hive" all the time without being stung by its immorality and vulgarity. They also know that the wasps of Satan love to hide between the covers of pornographic magazines, in lurid (and sometimes alluring) commercials and advertisements, in the all-pervasive materialistic and secular value system of their culture. They are always on the look out, ready to defend themselves against "the devil's schemes" which are so many and so creative.

Thank God for people who resist, who say, "I'm struggling to remain a Christian. I'm struggling to be the kind of person I ought to be. It isn't easy here. What should I do?"

You acknowledge the struggle and admit you need help. Then you gain strength by your willingness to take the next step:

### 3. Accept help

Now for the good news. You are not alone. Let's return to Ephesians 4, to verses 15 and 16:

> Instead, speaking the truth in love, we will in all things grow up into him who is the Head, that is, Christ. From him the whole body, joined and held together by every supporting ligament, grows and builds itself up in love, as each part does its work.

Why am I a Christian? Because I need help to become a better person.

Where does my help come from? It comes from the Lord who is the Head of the body, the Church:

> Because Christ Himself suffered when he was tempted, he is able to help those who are being tempted (Heb. 2:18).

When we give ourselves to Him, He who has already overcome temptation strengthens us as we do battle against it.

Do not take this assistance lightly. Keep praying to Him, keep in touch with Him, keep turning to and focusing on Him and He will give you victory.

Our help also comes from the church, from "every supporting ligament." The Christian glories in the company he keeps. He is not alone. He is upheld by his companions.

So many examples could be given of how this works. Having spent some time teaching on college campuses, I'll choose one about a young coed. The first time the sturdy young Christian bowed her head at the cafeteria breakfast table to give thanks the other girls snickered. When she raised her head she pleasantly asked what they were laughing at.

"You know," they said.

"Aren't you grateful?" she asked them.

"For what?" they asked.

"For your food."

"For our food, cafeteria food?" they laughed. "We bought it."

"Where did you get the money?"

"From our families."

"Where did they get it?"

"They worked for it."

"Where did they get the power to work?" She kept pushing her questions — quietly, kindly, but insistently, until she pushed them all the way back to the Source. They admitted there must be a God.

That evening two more joined her in saying grace. By the next evening, all six. Finally, the whole crowd joined her in a continuing prayer group. They became a Christian community on campus.[2]

Where does a single college woman get the courage to live out her Christian conviction before the snickers of her friends? From the Lord . . . and eventually from the community of believers. As soon as she took her stand, she helped others; in time, the help became mutual "supporting ligaments." This is how the church works. What commences as a solitary Christian walk soon becomes a parade of comrades helping each other on their pilgrimage.

### 4. Don't give up — give (yourself) away.

So don't give up in your desire to become a better you. The Lord and your fellow Christians will help you. There remains, though, one more suggestion I must mention. This is it: Give yourself away.

> From him the whole body, joined and held together by every supporting ligament, grows and builds itself up in love, *as each part does its work* (Eph. 4:16).

You have a work to do. What happens when you do your work? Go back up to verse 13:

> . . . until we all . . . become mature.

What does this maturity look like?

> . . . attaining to the whole measure of the fullness of Christ.

Maturity looks like Christ.

How will I know when I have reached full maturity, "to the whole measure of the fullness of Christ?" One answers the question with fear and trepidation, because the answer is so obvious: It has to do with a cross, and what

He did on it. He gave Himself away. For our sakes (see Phil. 2:5-11). You and I will know we're reaching maturity when we find ourselves giving us away for the sake of others.

Do you want to become a better person? There's no detour around this one. Jesus said it this way:

> For whoever wants to save his life will lose it, but whoever loses his life for me and for the gospel will save it (Mark 8:35).

There is no substitute for self-giving.

Kimberly Martin taught this lesson to a group of hardened convicts. When she was twenty-two months old, doctors gave her 24 hours to live. By a miracle, she fooled her doctors; her leukemia went into remission. She then underwent three years of chemotherapy, followed by a period of peace before she had a relapse which led to surgery and more chemotherapy at a cost far beyond her parent's ability to pay.

A reporter heard of Kimberly's plight and wrote the article which a few inmates in a maximum security prison in Pacific, Missouri read in their newspaper.

"We need to do something," they agreed. The warden granted permission for some fund raising. Then they asked to see her. Thus in the spring of 1983, some hard bitten prisoners lined up to meet her on Kimberly Martin Day, the first of her several visits to the prison.

One of the prisoners said, "Our problems suddenly seemed pretty petty compared to hers. Here we were healthy and alive, and this little girl didn't even know if she was going to be here next month." She wore a bonnet because her chemotherapy had left her bald. She was still so sick and weak that several times during her visit she had to go to the bathroom to throw up. But what this weak little girl did for those prisoners! One man said, "It really helped me to get involved and start caring again because you hardly ever see caring inside a prison. People get abused and killed and you don't even stop eating lunch."

On a later visit, a big, hulking, intimidating inmate knelt in front of her and gently said, "I'm the man you saw last time you were here who had the mohawk haircut and feather earring. I could tell you were afraid of me because of the way I looked. I've taken out my earring and grown my hair out so that you could see I'm not so mean looking after all."

She looked at him and smiled.

"See, I'm not so tough," 'Latif' Jones, 36 (serving a life term for double murder) confessed. "I just act tough because that's the way you have to be around here. So if you ever see me looking mean, just remember I'm pretending."

The newspaper article closed with this last sentence: "She gives us hope for our own future."[3] They forgot themselves for Kimberly's sake, and found themselves. They gave themselves away — and found love and hope.

Kimberly's is like a secular version of the Christmas story isn't it? Remember when a little child came to men and women imprisoned by sin, locked up in their tiny little egos, having lost the life they so desperately grasped? God freed them and, through the love of the Child, made them better.

This is how to become a better person: Look to Jesus, accept Him, follow Him, imitate Him, and you will become more and more like Him who is the very best person of all.

Ephesians 4:11-16; 6:1-13
Philippians 2:5-11
Hebrews 12:1-2
II Peter 3:11-12a
I John 1:8-10

**Endnotes**

**1.** Charles R. Swindoll, *Living on the Ragged Edge*. Waco, Texas: Word Books, co. 1985, pp. 148, 149.

**2.** Samuel M. Shoemaker, *By the Power of God*, New York: Harper and Brothers, pp. 146-147.

**3.** Christopher Phillips, "How 1000 Convicts Changed a Little Girl's Life and How She Changed Theirs," *Parade Magazine*, 2/28/88, pp. 10, 13.